I0113557

R. S. Ashton

The Christian Traveller's Continental Handbook

R. S. Ashton

The Christian Traveller's Continental Handbook

ISBN/EAN: 9783337026530

Printed in Europe, USA, Canada, Australia, Japan

Cover: Foto ©Andreas Hilbeck / pixelio.de

More available books at **www.hansebooks.com**

THE

CHRISTIAN TRAVELLER'S

Continental Handbook.

EDITED BY THE

REV. R. S. ASHTON, B.A.,

FOURTH EDITION, ENLARGED.

LONDON :
ELLIOT STOCK, 62, PATERNOSTER ROW, E.C.
1889.

PREFACE.

A FOURTH edition of this Handbook is offered to the travelling public in the assurance that it meets a felt want. Considerable alterations have been made, with a view to render it more useful. And while believing that, if the list of abbreviations on page xii. is carefully noted, the book will explain itself, the Editor would bespeak attention for the Introduction, in which the object of the book is stated, and the new features of this edition are explained.

R. S. ASHTON,
Secretary of Evangelical Continental Society.

13, BLOMFIELD STREET,
LONDON WALL, E.C.

CONTENTS.

INTRODUCTION.

I.—THE chief aim of this Handbook is to direct attention to Evangelistic and other operations on the Conti-
nent, and to facilitate a visit to some of them. In the
case of France, several short tours have been sketched
out. Before undertaking any of these, it would be well
to obtain still more precise information respecting hours
of meeting, etc., from the secretaries of the societies to
which the stations belong, or from a pastor living in the
town which forms the starting-point. All such applica-
tions may be made in English. Any attempt to present
precise information would probably be misleading, owing
to the frequent changes incident to such work.

II.—English services are indicated, and the towns in
which they are held are printed in heavier type, so as to
strike the eye. In regard to the permanent chaplaincies,
the name of the minister is given in most cases, and the
address of the church and the hours of service. For the
summer chaplaincies only the place is given as a rule,
the traveller being referred for other information to the
announcements now to be found in all the principal
hotels.

III.—For travellers desirous of visiting scenes rendered
memorable by events in Protestant history, several tours
are sketched out. This is a tentative effort which in

future editions may be extended, should it meet with general approval.

IV.—In regard to Germany, a general view of Protestant Inner Mission Agencies is given ; also a list of the chief Protestant universities, with the names of a few of the principal professors. The chapter on ' Würtemberg,' the details of which were kindly given by friends on the spot, will, it is hoped, interest some.

V.—At the great General Missionary Conference of last year it was felt desirable to omit all details of missions to Roman Catholics, and of the societies in England and America that either have missions of their own in Europe or that help the societies established in the various countries. This deficiency is in some measure supplied by the information given here.

As this Handbook was *started by, and is still published largely at the expense of, the Evangelical Continental Society*, we begin with a reference to its operations. By grants made to French, Belgian, and Italian Evangelical Societies, and by securing the services of faithful men, placed under due supervision in Spain and Bohemia, it has rendered great help for more than forty years. It was established, and is still conducted, on *undenominational* principles.

The Foreign Aid Society, a few years older than the Evangelical Continental Society, is carried on on similar principles. Its supporters are mainly found in the Church of England.

VI.—Sunday Schools are to be found in most towns where active religious life exists, and a visit to the various churches will enable the traveller to ascertain the hour when the children assemble, if the same is not indicated in the following pages. But if any persons are desirous of getting fuller information, they may do so by applying to the gentlemen whose names will be found in the list that appears at the end of this Handbook.

Societies, etc., on the Continent with which the Evangelical Continental Society is connected.

Soc. Evangélique de France.
Union des Eglises Evangéliques Libres de France.
McAll Mission.
Soc. Evangélique Belge.
Free Christian Church of Italy.
Waldensian Church.
Rev. W. H. Gulick (A. B. C. F. M.), San Sebastian, Spain.
Pastor Scholtesz, Krabschitz, bei Raudnitz, Bohemia.

Other British Societies Engaged in the Work of Continental Evangelization.

Foreign Evangelization Society. Secretary, Rev. Horace Noel, Woking.
Spanish Evangelization Society. Treasurer, Mrs. R. Peddie, 2, Granville Terrace, Merchiston, Edinburgh.
Spanish and Portuguese Church Aid Society. Secretary, Rev. L. S. Tugwell, 8, Adam Street, Strand, W.C.
Waldensian Missions' Aid Society. Secretary, Captain Frobisher, 118, Pall Mall, S.W.
Wesleyan Missionary Society, Centenary Hall, Bishopsgate Street.
Baptist Missionary Society, Furnival Street, Holborn.
British and Foreign Bible Society, 146, Queen Victoria Street, E.C.
National Bible Society of Scotland, Glasgow and Edinburgh.
Religious Tract Society, 56, Paternoster Row, E.C.
Sunday School Union, 56, Old Bailey, E.C.
London Society for Promoting Christianity among the Jews, 16, Lincoln's Inn Fields, W.C.
British Society for Propagation of the Gospel among the Jews, 96, Great Russell Street, W.C.
Free Church of Scotland Missions to the Jews, Free Church Offices, The Mound, Edinburgh.
British and Foreign Sailors' Society, Sailors' Institute, Mercer Street, Shadwell, E.
Free Church of Scotland Continental Committee, Free Church Offices, The Mound, Edinburgh.

American Societies, etc., engaged in the same Work.

American Board of Commissioners for Foreign Missions, Boston.
Methodist Episcopal Church, Foreign Missions of, New York.
Baptist Missionary Society, Boston.
Foreign Sunday School Association, Brooklyn, U.S.

ABBREVIATIONS USED IN THIS GUIDE.

C. and C.C.S. Colonial and Continental Church Society—English Services.

S.P.G. Society for Propagation of Gospel in Foreign Parts—English Services.

Engl. Episc. Ch. English Episcopal Church.

Presb. Ch. Presbyterian Church.

Meth. or Wesl. Ch. Wesleyan Chapel.

Bapt. Ch. Baptist Chapel.

Meth. Episc. Ch. Methodist Episcopal Church of America.

Amer. American.

Y.M.C.A. Young Men's Christian Association.

A.B.C.F.M. American Board of Commissioners for Foreign Missions.

The figures after name and address of Churches signify the hours of Service.

FRANCE.

Population (1886), 38,218,903. Protestants about 800,000.

EXPLANATIONS, ETC.

Ref. Ch.—*Eglise Réformée Nationale.* With 101 consistories and over 700 pastors. Secy. of Commission Permanente, M. Aimé Couve, Avocat, Marseille.

Luth. Ch.—*Eglise Luthérienne ou de la Confession d'Augsbourg.* With 6 consistories and 98 pastors. Commission Exécutive, Secy. M. H. Lambert, Bourg-la-Reine (Seine).

Free Ch.—*Union des Eglises Evangéliques Libres.* With 42 pastors and 7 Evangelists. Secy. of Commission Synodale, M. Meyreuis, 3, Rue Pierre-le-Grand, Paris.

Meth. Ch.—*Eglise Evangélique Méthodiste.* With 139 places of worship, 30 pastors, 10 evangelists and teachers, and 105 lay-preachers. Secy. of Conférence, Past. M. Gallienne, Nîmes.

Methodist Missions.—11 chapels and 19 preaching places. Supt., Rev. W. Gibson, 86, Bould. de Versailles, St. Cloud.

Bapt. Ch.—*Eglises Baptistes.* 17 pastors and evangelists.

Soc. Centr.—*Société Centrale.* (Ref. Ch.) Secy., Past. Duchemin, 75, Rue des Batignolles, Paris. 83 stations and 2 Preparatory Theol. Schs.—1. Paris, 103, Rue Nollet; 2. Tournon, near Valence.

Soc. Ev. Fr.—*Société Evangélique de France* (undenominational). Secy., Past. Mouron, 76, Rue d'Assas, Paris. 25 stations, 15 schools, and 77 annexes.

Commission d'Evangélisation of Free Churches. 20 stations. Treasurer, M. P. Guignard, Chât. du Barrail, Ste-Foy-la-Grande (Gironde).

Mission Intérieure, Comité Parisien. Employs Lecturers. Now affiliated with *Soc. Centrale.*

Soc. Ev. Gen.—*Société Evangélique de Genève.* See under head of Geneva. 12 stations and 60 colporteurs.

The McAll Mission has 44 stations in Paris and 79 in the Departments, besides 4 in Algiers and Tunis, and 1 in Corsica. Honorary President, Rev. Dr. McAll, 28, Villa Molitor, Auteuil, Paris. Mission Bureau: Finance Secy., M. W. Soltau, 28, Villa Molitor, Auteuil, Paris.

Salvation Army.—Maréchale Booth-Clibborn, 3, Rue Auber. 3 Divisions: Paris (3 stations), South (15 stations), and Southeast (13 stations); with a section in the West (4 stations), and another in the Tarn (4 stations).

1

Aix-les-Bains.—C. and C.C.S. (April to Oct.) St. Swithins. Presb. Ch., May and June and Aug. 15 to Oct. 15, 11 a.m. Ref. Ch., services at the Asile Evangélique at 3, from May 15 to Oct. 15.

Amiens.—Protestants 709. Ref. Ch., 47, Rue de Metz, 11 ; S. Sch., 10.

Anduze.—Protestants 4,600. Ref. Ch., Pl. de Brie, at 11, and Chap. de l'Asile de Bon Secours, at 4 in summer. Meth. Ch., Route de St. Félix, at 2. 'Brethren' Service, Rue du Pont, at 10.

Angers.—Ref. Ch. Rue du Musée, 12. The building dates from the 12th century. Free Ch., 33, Rue Toussaint, at 11 in summer ; S. Sch. at 10 a.m.

Antibes.—Ch. of Engld., Rev. D. Simpson. At the Cap ; St. Ann's. French serv. at Jûan les Pons, 2.30.

Arcachon.—C. and C.C.S. St. Thomas' Ch. Rev. S. Radcliff. Ref. Ch., R. du Temple, 10 a.m. Bible Dépôt, Past. Paul Monod, 37, Av. Gambetta.

Argelès.—S.P.G. March to June.

Avignon.—Ref. Ch., Rue Joseph Vernet, 10.30. Bible Dépôt, Quartier St. Ruff, Pavillon Fayette.

Avranches.—English Episcopal Church.

Bagnères de Bigorre.—Ref. Ch., Avenue de Salut, 3 ; S. Sch., 2.

Bagnères de Luchon.—Ref. Ch., Chap. de la Villa Corneille, Allée de Piqué (in summer only), 1.

Bar-le-Duc.—Ref. Ch., Rue du Gué, 10 and 2.

Barnave.—Ref. Ch. Evangelization in the Diois. Director, Past. Marzials.

Bayonne.—Ref. Ch., Rue Vainsot, 10.30.

Besançon.—Protestants 6,500. Ref. Ch., 4, Rue des Remparts, 10. Bible Dépôt, Les Founottes.

Beuzeval.—C. and C.C.S. Services in Egl. Evangélique, Rev. J. N. Soden. French Services in the season. Maison Evangélique (Protestant Sea-bathing Establishment).

Biarritz.—C. and C.C.S. St. Andrew's, Rev. G. E. Broade. Presb. Ch., at Fr. Prot. Ch., 11 and 3. Nov. to April. Bible Dépôt, Villa Shakspere.

Bordeaux.—C. and C.C.S., Rev. J. W. L. Burke. Protestants 8,500. Ref. Ch., 12, Rue Notre Dame, 12 in winter, and 10.30 in summer ; also at 32, Rue du Hâ, at 10.30, except in summer, and then at 9 a.m. 28, Rue Lavelle-Fatin (La Bastide), 4. Free Ch., 17, Rue Barennes, 12.30 and 7.30.

McAll Mission, Director M. Chas. Chaigne, 20, Rue Despurmel. 6, Stations : principal one, 2, Cours St. Louis, Les Chartreux.

Salvation Army, Western Division—Capt. Fornachon, 9, Rue du Hautoir.

Protestant Bookseller, H. Muller.

Boulogne.—C. and C.C.S. Trinity Ch., Rev. E. R. Parr. S.P.G. St. John's, Rev. J. H. Fry. Engl. Wesleyan Ch., R. de l'Ancienne Comédie, 11 and 7, S. Sch., 3. Rev. W. J. J. Barkell.

Ref. Ch., 15, Rue St. Martin, 11 and 7.30.

Bible and Tract Dépôt, Past. Dégremont, 54 Bould. du Prince Albert.

McAll Mission, 53, Rue Ad. Thiers, and another.

BOURGES (Cher).—Ref. Ch., Avenue de la Gare, 11. Service also at Asnières-les-Bourges, 2 p.m.

BREST.—Ref. Ch., Rue d'Aguillon, at 11. Bible Dépôt, 198, R. de la Vierge.

Bride-les-Bains (Savoy). C. and C.C.S.

Caen.—S.P.G. St. Michael's Rev. B. Ring. Ref. Ch., Rue de Géôle, 11.30. Bethel on Quay. Bible Dépôt, Past. Bourgeon, 60, R. Bosnieres.

Calais.—C. and C.C.S. Trinity, Rev. St. J. F. Mitchell. Engl. Wesleyan Ch., Rue du Temple, 11 and 6.30.

Fr. Meth. Ch., Rue Pont Lottin, 11 and 6.

Bible Dépôt and Evangelical Books and Tracts, Mr. Sisling, 76, Rue Lafayette.

McAll Mission, 6, Rue Françia.

Cannes.—English Episcopal Church. (1) Christ Church, and (2) Trinity (C. and C.C.S., Rev. W. Brookes) and (3) St. Paul's.

CANNES :
Presb. Church, Route de Fréjus, 11 and 3. Rev. W.
P. Minto. Nov. to April.
Egl. Ref. Evang., Route de Grasse. Pasteur Marrauld,
R. de Fréjus, 44.
Egl. Evang. Française, R. Notre Dame. Pasteur Farjat,
Villa Lisnard, Av. de Windsor.
German Church, Bould. du Cannet.
Bible Dépôt, 6, R. des Marchés.
Asile Evangélique, Route de Grasse. A Convalescent
Home and Hospital.
Home for Servants, Bould. du Cannet. Hospice mari-
time de l'Enfance, 40 Children, Sq. Brougham.
Ladies' Home for Invalids.
Town Mission Salle, Rue Ste. Marguerite.
McAll Mission, 6, R. du Marché. Director, M. Hy.
Webber.
Cauterets.—C. and C.C.S. Ref. Ch., Rue de la Raillière,
in the season at 1.
CETTE.—Ref. Ch., 32, Rue Neuve du Nord, 10.30.
McAll Mission, 3, R. l'Issanka.
Le Lazaret, open from June 25 to Aug. 30—asylum for
Protestant poor requiring sea baths.
CHAMBÉRI.—Ref. Ch., Rue de la Banque, 10.
Chantilly.—C. and C.C.S., Rev. T. Mackmurdo.
Engl. Meth. Ch., Route de Paris, 7.30. French
at 2.45.
Cherbourg.—C. and C.C.S. serv. in Egl. Evang. Ref.
Ch., Place Divette, 11 ; S. Sch. at 10.
McAll Mission, 72, Quai de Paris.
Bible Dépôt, Lebel, Rue St. Sauveur, à Octeville.
CLERMONT FERRAND (Puy de Dôme).—Ref. Ch., Rue
Sidoine Appollinaire, at 1.
Free Ch., Rue Hte. St. André, at 1.
COGNAC.—Protestants (in 14 communes) 400. Ref. Ch.,
Rue du Temple, at 12.
Compiègne.—C. and C.C.S. St. Andrew's. Rev. J.
Thomson.

Contrexéville (Vosges).—S.P.G. June to Aug.

Creil.—Engl. Meth. Ch., 3.30. Ref. Ch., Rue Chas. Brobeil, 4.

Dieppe.—S.P.G., All Saints, Rev. G. Gibson. C. and C.C.S., Christ Ch., Rue Asseline, Rev. A. F. W. Wilkinson. Ref. Ch., Rue de la Barre, at 11. Bible Dépôt, Faure, Cordonnier, R. St. Réoni.

DIEU-LE-FIT (Drôme).—Ref. Ch. Normal School (*Ecole Modèle*). Meth. Ch. at 2 p.m.

DIJON.—Protestants 800. Ref. Ch. Services held in old chapel of the Palais des Etats, now the Hôtel de Ville —entrance Rue Condé—at 10.

Dinan.—S.P.G., Christ Church, Rev. J. G. Orger. Ref. Ch., Services in Engl. Ch. on Sunday evening.

Dunkirk.—C. and C.C.S., Rev. A. Rust. Ref. Ch., Quai au Bois, 11. Seamen's Institute.

Eaux Chaudes.—C. and C.C.S. Also French service in the season.

EPERNAY.—Prot. Ch., Rue de la Poterne, 12.

Etretat.—C. and C.C.S., Rev. J. N. Soden.

ELBŒUF.—Protestant pop. 1,000. Ref. Ch., Temple Protestant, Rue de Constantine, 10.30. Lutheran Ch. and Schs., 18, Av. Gambetta, at 10 French, and 2 German, fortnightly. Wesly. Evangelistic Mgs., Rue Caudebec, Wednesday, 8 p.m.

FERNEY, near Geneva.—Temple at end of the town on the road to Voltaire's Château ; also two orphanages. Evangelization carried on in this district under direction of Pasteur Pasquet.

FONTAINEBLEAU.—Ref. Ch., 3, Rue Béranger, 10.30.

Golfe Juan.—C. and C.C.S. in winter.

Grasse.—C. and C.C.S. in winter, Rev. H. E. Gedge.

GRENOBLE.—Ref. Ch., Rue Lesdiguières, 10.30. French services in the season at Allevard, Temple, Pl. du Nord, 12 ; and at Uriage, in the Grand Châlet, at 4.

McAll Mission, 33, Rue de la Fédération.

Guines.—C. and C.C.S. Rev. St. J. F. Mitchell.

Hâvre.—Engl. Ep. Ch., Holy Trinity, Rue Mexico. Rev. H. S. Cheshire, 31, R. Ste. Adresse. About 6,000 Protestants. Ref. Ch., Grand Temple, Rue du Lycée, 10.30. French Services also conducted every other Sunday by best known evangelical pastors from Paris, etc., in Ch. in R. de la Paix, 10.15. Meth. Ch., 16, Rue de l'Hôpital. English at 11 and 6.30. Rev. G. Whelpton. Also French at 4, and Evangelistic Meeting at 8.

Large Sailors' Home, 63, Rue Dauphine. Mgs., Mon., Thurs., and Saty., 7.45 p.m.

Missions to Seamen (Ch. of Engld.), Reading-room. Serv. at 7.30 p.m.

Meetings for Bretons in Breton at 63, R. Dauphine, Sunday and Wedy., 8 p.m.

United Prayer Meeting for Christian Workers at house of Mme. Delacroix, 157, Bould. de Strasbourg, Saty., 5 p.m.

Bible Dépôt, 20, R. Bard.

Honfleur.—C. and C.C.S. Engl. Ch., various. French service once a month in Engl. Ch. on alternate Sundays at 3. Sailors' Home, Rue de la Gare. Engl. Services, 11 and 7.

Hyères.—C. and C.C.S. St. Paul's, Rev. R. J. Karney, in winter. Bible Dépôt, Gueret, Pl. des Palmiers.

Ile de la Croix.—Ch. of Eng., 11 and 3, Rev. H. Smythe.

La-Force (Dordogne, viâ Libourne).—John Bost's establishments. Director, Pasteur Rayroux. Eight asylums for orphans, blind, idiots, etc.

La Rochelle.—Protestants 1,000. Ref. Ch., Rue de la Ferté, 12.

McAll Mission, 6, Rue du Temple.

La Roche-sur-Yon.—Temple, Rue Chanzy, 10 a.m.

Le Mans.—Ref. Ch., Rue du Bourg-Belé, at 10.

Lille.—C. and C.C.S. Christ Ch., Rev. W. Burnet, 10.30 and 6.30, and services at Armentières.

Protestants 2,000. Ref. Ch. Rue Jeanne d'Arc, Place du Temple, 11, and S. Sch. at 10.

LILLE :
McAll Mission, Rue du Faubg. de Tournai, Fives.
Bible Dépôt, 6, Rue Brigode.
LISIEUX.—Meth. Ch., 10.30 and 7.30.
LORIENT.—Ref. Ch., 10. Evangelization. Director,
Pastor Kissel.
Bible Dépôt, Kerentrech-Calvin, Mme. Muller.
Luchon.—C. and C.C.S. M. Corneille's Chapel.
Lyons.—C. and C.C.S. Holy Trinity, 1, Rue Godefroy,
Rev. H. Lister.
Protestants 14,000. Ref. Ch., Place du Change, 11 ;
and 6, Quai de la Guillotière, 9 a.m. Luth. Ch., 2,
Rue de Pavia. French Service ; German Service.
Free Ch., 10, Rue Lanterne, 10.30. Stations : (1) 22,
Gde. Rue de Cuire, à la Croix Rousse, Sunday, 7 p.m.;
(2) 89, Avenue de Saxe, Sunday, 8 p.m.
Bapt. Ch., 78, Rue Bugeaud, 10 and 4.
McAll Mission, four stations—one at 89, Avenue de
Saxe, Les Brotteaux. Director, M. le Past. Dubus,
20, Rue Godefroy.
Bible and Tract Dépôt, 10, Rue Lanterne.
Protestant Bookseller, H. Georg, Place de la Républi-
que.
Infirmerie Protestante Evangélique, 2, Rue Dupont,
Croix Rousse. Private rooms for strangers at 6 frs.
per day.
Y.M.C.A., 6, Quai de Retz. B. class, Friday, 8.30 p.m.
Soldiers' Reading Room, 12, R. Thermes.
Comité Protestant de Lyon—President, M. E. Milsom,
and Treasurer, M. R. de Cazenove, 8, Rue Sala—
employs Evangelists, etc., in the Hautes Alpes
and in the Basses Alpes.
MACON.—Free Ch., 3, Rue Joséphine, 10 ; S. Sch. at 1.
Bible Dépôt, 3, Rue Joséphine.
Marseilles.—Protestants 14,000.
Eng. Ch., 100, Rue Sylvabelle, 10.30 and 3. Rev. T. C.
Skeggs.
Ref. Ch., Temples : 15, Rue Grignan ; 15, Rue Delille ;

MARSEILLES :

and 2, Rue Vincent. Services at 10. S. Sch. at 9 in each Temple.

Free Ch., 133, Cours Lieutaud, at 10 and 2.30.

McAll Mission, 6 stations : principal one, 38, Rue de la République, Sunday and Friday, 8.30. Director, Past. Em. Lenoir, 72, Rue St. Jacques.

Salvation Army, 61, Rue Fortune.

Ecole Pratique d'Evangélisation. Director, M. le Pasteur Richard, 75, Rue St. Jacques.

Y.M.C.A., 87, Vieux Chemin de Rome.

Strangers' Rests and Miss. to For. Seamen, 38, Quai du Port. Director, Mr. Faithfull.

Sailors' Home, 104, Rue de la République. Sunday service, 7.30.

Bible, etc., Dépôt, 38, Rue de la République.

MEAUX.—Ref. Ch., Place du Temple, 10.30.

MELUN.—Ref. Ch., 15, Rue Notre Dame, 3.30. McAll Mission.

Mentone.—Christ Ch., East Bay (C. and C.C.S.), in winter, St. John's, West Bay (S.P.G.), Sept. to June, Rev. H. Sidebotham.

Presb. Ch. at Hall les Grottes, East Bay, at 11, Rev. J. E. Somerville (in winter).

French Evang. Ch., Rue du Castellar. Oct. to July. Pasteur Delapierre.

German Ch., Avenue Urbana. Nov. to April.

McAll Mission, 2 stns. Director, M. J. Anderson.

Clergyman's Home.

Villa Helvétia, Home for Invalid Ladies. Supt. Miss Armstrong.

Bible and Tract Dépôt, Laurente, Gde. Rue.

MONTAUBAN.—Protestants 3,100. Ref. Ch. 3 Temples.

Egl. Réf. Indépendante, at Temple de la Faculté.

McAll Mission, 95, R. Lacapelle.

Protestant Theological Faculty. Profs. Bois, Doumergue, Bruston, and others.

Protestant Bookseller and Bible Dépôt, Mme. Laborde, 14, Pl. de la Préfecture.

MONTBÉLIARD.—(A Lutheran district.) 3 Lutheran Churches. Bapt. Ch., Oratoire.
Bible Dépôt, Meister, Pl. de la Préfecture.
Mont Dore.—S.P.G. In August.
MONTPELLIER.—Ref. Ch., Rue Maguelonne, 10.
Egl. Ev. Indépendante.
Bible Dépôt, Bould. Strasbourg, Maison Briet.
McAll Mission, 29, Cours des Casernes.
MORLAIX.—Bapt. Ch. Pastor, A. Jenkins. Services in French at 10 and in Breton at 7 p.m.
NANCY.—Protestants 2,400. Ref. Ch., Place St. Jean, 9 in German and at 10 in French.
Meth. Ch., 6bis, Rue Ste. Anne, 10.30.
McAll Mission, 41, Rue de la Gde., Biesse, Morristown.
Nantes.—English Episcopal Ch. at British Consulate.
Ref. Ch., Pl. de Gigant, 12 ; S. Sch. at 9 a.m.
Nice.—English Episcopal Church. Presb. Ch., 14, Rue St. Etienne, at 10.30 and 3. Rev. Dr. Murray Mitchell. Amer. Episcopal Church.
Luth. Ch. (French), Rue d'Augsbourg, 10.30.
Vaudois Ch., 50, Rue Gioffreddo. Pastor, A. Malan.
Asile Evangélique, Ruelle des Prés.
Bible Dépôt, 47, Av. de la Gare.
McAll Mission, 3 stns. : chief one, 47, Avenue de la Gare. Director, M. le Past. Borel.
Italian Evangelization, Rue de Villefranche. Pasteur Petraí, 50, R. Gioffreddo.
NÎMES.—Protestants 15,540. Three Ref. Chs.
(1) Grand Temple, Bd. des Calquières, 10.30.
(2) Petit Temple, Ru due Grand Couvent, 8.30 and 10.30 a.m. S. School, 1.30.
(3) L'Oratoire, Pl. de l'Oratoire, 9.30 a.m.
Free Ch., Rue du Fort, 9.30. S. Sch. 1.30.
Meth. Ch., Rue St. Dominique, 9 and 3.
Brethren's Meeting, Rue Grétry.
Religious Service, at *Maison de Santé*, Quai de la Fontaine, 4 p.m. Every Sunday.
Salvation Army, Southern Division, Major G. Le Cornu,

NIMES :

    26, Rue Notre-Dame. Sunday, 8 a.m. and 8 p.m., and Friday, 8 p.m.

    Y. M.C.A., 8, Place de la Bouquerie.

    Normal School for Female Teachers, Rue des Flottes. Seven Ladies' Boarding Schools—one of them a Wesleyan Establishment.

    Maison de Santé (Sick and Infirm Women). Orphe·linat (Filles).

Orleans.—English Episcopal Ch. Ref. Ch., Pl. St. Pierre en Pont, near the Cathedral, 12 ; Evening Service, at 8 in Presbytère, near Temple (no Evening Service in Aug.) ; S. Sch. at 11.

ORTHEZ.—Protestants 1,550. Ref. Ch., Rue des Innocents, 10.30. Free Ch. Brethren Service.

PARIS.

Protestants 40,000.

Eng. Episc. Ch. (1) Faubourg St. Honoré.   5, Rue d'Aguesseau (C. and C.C.S.), 11, 3.30, and 8. Rev. T. Howard Gill.

(2) 30, Rue des Bassins, 10 and 3. Rev. W. Washington.

(3) Christ Church, Neuilly, 11 and 4.   Rev. R. de Carteret.

Congreg. Ch., 23, Rue Royale, 11.15 and 7.30.   Rev. 3. H. Anderson.

Engl. Wesl. Ch., 4, Rue Roquépine, 41, Boulevard Malesherbes, 11.30 and 7.30 ; and 16, Rue Demours aux Ternes, at 3.30. Revs. W. Gibson and T. Bramley Hart.

Scotch Ch., R. Bayard, 11 and 3.   Rev. P. Beaton.

Amer. Episc. Ch., 7, Avenue de l'Alma, 11 and 4.   Rev. Dr. Morgan.

Amer. Union Ch., 21, Rue de Berri, 11.   Rev. Dr. Thurber.

Ref. Ch. (1) L'Oratoire, 147, Rue St. Honoré, at noon.

(2) Ste. Marie, 216, Rue St. Antoine, at noon.

(3) St. Esprit, 5, Rue Roquépine, 10.

PARIS :

(4) Pentemont, Rue de Grenelle, at noon.

(5) L'Etoile, 54, Avenue de la Grande Armée, 10 and 4.

(6) Passy, 65, Rue des Sablons, 10 ; and other Chs.

Luth. Ch. (1) La Rédemption, 16, Rue Chauchat, at 10.15.

(2) Les Billettes, 18, Rue des Billettes, at noon ; and other Churches.

Free Chs. (1) Eglise Taitbout, 42, Rue de Provence, 10.

(2) Egl. du Luxembourg, 58, Rue Madame, 10.30 and 8.

(3) Eglise du Nord, Rue des Petits Hôtels, 10.

(4) Eglise du Centre, 115, R. du Temple, 11 and 8.

Bapt. Ch., 48, Rue de Lille, 1.

Meth. Chs. (1) 4, Rue Roquépine, 2.30 and 8.

(2) Chapelle des Ternes, 16, Rue Demours, 12 and 8.

Prot. Theological Faculty, 83, Bd. Arago. Profs. Lichtenberger, Sabatier, Ménégoz, Viguié, etc.

McAll Mission Services. The principal stations in the Capital are La Concorde, 23, Rue Royale, near the Madeleine, every week evening at 8.15, Sundays, 4.30 ; Salle Rivoli, 104, Rue St. Antoine, near Hôtel de Ville, every evening, 8 ; 8, Boulevard Bonne Nouvelle, every evening, 8.15; 133, Rue St. Denis, near Halles Centrales, every evening, except Monday, at 8.

Methodist Evangelistic Mission, Sunday Evening Conférences, at 8 p.m., 39, Bd. des Capucines. Also Evangelistic Meetings at 6, Rue de l'Abbé de l'Epée, near Panthéon, Sunday evening at 8 p.m. Other rooms at St. Ouen, St. Denis, St. Cloud, Argenteuil and Asnières.

Bapt. Evangelistic Mission—Meetings at R. du Texel and 13, R. de Buce. Sunday at 8. Director, Past. Ph. Vincent, 104, Bould. de Vaugirard.

Salvation Army, Major Jeanmonod, 187, Quai Valmy, Sunday at 3 and 8.15 ; at Rue Auber 3, and at Belleville.

Œuvre des Affligés. Pastor Armand Delille's Mission, 85, Avenue Michelet, near St. Ouen Cemetery, Sunday,

Paris :

Monday and Thursday, 3 to 5 in summer, 2 to 4 in winter. Also every day at 23, Rue Royale, 2.30.

Mlle. de Brōen's Mission. Meetings in Iron Room, 32, Rue Bolivar (Belleville), Sunday, 3.30 and 8.30. Mission-House, at 3, Rue Clavel. Medical Mission.

London Jews' Society, M. L. C. Mamlock, 119, Rue de Rome.

Young Men's Christian Association—*Union Centrale*— 4, Faubg. Montmartre. Rooms, etc., open from 10 to 10. Treasurer, M. E. Poulain, 60, Rue d'Aboukir.

Y.M.C.A., English, 160, R. Montmartre. Sunday, 4.30. President, H. Skepper, Esq.

Deaconesses' Institution, 95, Rue de Reuilly. Service on Sunday, 3.30. Central Establishment at Clermont (Oise).

Soc. de l'Histoire du Protestantisme Français. Secretary, M. Jules Bonnet, 5, Rue du Champ Royal, Courbevoie (Seine).

The Library of this Society is at 54, Rue des Saints-Pères, and is open to the public on Monday, Tuesday, Wednesday, and Thursday, from 1 to 5.

Orphanages (Girls), at 63, Rue Pernetty, Plaisance ; and 15, Rue Clairaut, Batignolles.

Do. (Boys), 41, Avenue Victor Hugo.

Asile de la Muette (Old Men), 91, Rue des Boulets, La Roquette.

Asile de Bon Secours (Old Men, Lutheran Ch.), 99, Rue de Charonne.

Mission Evangélique aux Femmes de la Classe Ouvrière, 179, Rue Daguerre. Directress, Madame Dalencourt, 75, Rue Escudier, Boulogne-s.-Seine.

Dépôt for Rel. Tract Soc., 4, Pl. du Théâtre Français, Palais Royal. Another Dépôt, 33, Rue des Saints-Pères.

B. and F. Bible Society, M. G. Monod, 58, Rue de Clichy.

Evangl. Alliance, French Branch. Secy., Past. Théod. Monod, 36, Bould. Henri IV.

PARIS :

Œuvre Evangélique du Quartier St. Marcel (Lutheran), 19, Rue Tournefort.

Société Biblique Protestante de Paris. Agent Général, M. le Pasteur Douen, 54, Rue des Saints-Pères.

Société Biblique de France. Agent Général, M. le Pasteur F. Vermeil, 22, Rue d'Astorg.

Société des Traités Religieux. Agent Général, M. le Pasteur Arbousse-Bastide, 33, Rue des Saints-Pères.

Société des Ecoles du Dimanche. Président, M. le Pasteur Paumier, 74, Rue de l'Université.

Paris City Mission—*Comité Auxiliaire d'Evangélisation de Paris.* Secretary, Mr. Lockie, 71, Rue de Batignolles. 8 Agents.

Com. d'Evangélisation d'Israel de Paris. President, Pasteur Banzet, 13, Rue Michelet.

Soc. des Missions Evangéliques (Lessouto, Senegal, Tahiti, etc.). Maison des Missions, 26, Rue des Fossés St. Jacques. Directeur, M. le Pasteur Bœgner.

Société de Tempérance de la Croix Bleue. Secretary, M. D. Ludwig, 73, Rue Laugier.

Comité Parisien pour le Relèvement de la Moralité Publique. Secretary, M. le Pasteur Fallot, 17, Rue des Petits-Hôtels.

Œuvre de la Chaussée-du-Maine, 74, R. des Fourneaux, Ouvroirs, Asile, etc. Inquire of Mme. de Pressensé, 9, R. du Val-de-Grâce.

Œuvre des Jeunes Filles de Magasin. 27, Rue J. Jacques Rousseau, open from 12 to 10.

Protestant Booksellers :—Grassart, 2, Rue de la Paix ; Fischbacher, 33, Rue de Seine ; Monnerat, 48, Rue de Lille ; Chastel, 4, Rue Roquépine ; Voreaux, 14, Rue Chauveau-Lagarde ; Sandoz and Thuillier. 4, Rue de Tournon.

Large Roman Catholic Institutions :—

Œuvre des Petites Sœurs des Pauvres. 5 Establishments in Paris, one in Rue St. Jacques. In 1885 there

PARIS :

were in France and other lands 242 houses served by 4,000 sisters, and giving shelter to 27,000 old men.

Frères de St. Jean de Dieu. Rue Lecourbe, Vaugirard Asylum for scrofulous children.

Abbé Roussel's Orphanage for Boys.   40, Rue de la Fontaine, Auteuil.

Cancer Hospital.   Rue Lourmel, near Bould. de Grenelle, kept by the *Dames du Calvaire.*

Hospitalité du Travail.   Temporary Home for Destitute at Auteuil.   Directed by nuns of Notre-Dame de Calvaire.

Asiles de Nuit.   9, Rue de Tocqueville, and 14, Bould. de Vaugirard (for men).   253, Rue St. Jacques (for women).

ENVIRONS OF PARIS.

Asnières.—Meth. Ch., 24, Avenue de Courbevoie, 10.30 ; English Service, 3.

Boulogne-s.-Seine.—Ref. Ch., 117, Route de la Reine, 1.30 ; S. Sch., 10.

Courbevoie.—Asile Lambrecht, 46, Rue de Colombes, for Old Men and Children.   French Service, Sunday 10.

Nanterre.—Asile (Women and Little Children), 5, Rue St. Denis.

Neuilly.—Maison de Santé (Men), 57, Bd. Bineau.

Puteaux.—Lutheran Ch., Rue de Paris, 12.30.

St. Germain-en-Laye. — Ref. Ch., Avenue des Loges Grille de Pontoise.   May 1 to Sept. 30, 10 a.m. ; Oct. 1 to April 30, 1.30.

St. Cloud.—Engl. Wesl. Ch., 7, Bould. de Versailles, 11.

Versailles.—C. and C.C.S., Engl. Ch., Rev. J. Peck. Ref. Ch., 3, Rue Hoche, 10.

McAll Mission, 81, R. de la Paroisse.

Pau.—C. and C.C.S., Trinity, Rev. J. H. Rogers, and S.P.G., St. Andrew's, Rev. R. H. D. Acland-Troyte,

PAU :

Oct. to May. Presb. Ch., Av. du Gd. Hôtel, 11 and
3, Rev. G. Brown, Oct. to June. Protestants 800.
Ref. Ch., Rue Serviez, 2 ; S. Sch., 9. Free Ch., 5,
Passage de Ségur, 9.30 and 1.30.

POITIERS.—Ref. Ch., 5, Rue des Ecossais.
McAll Mission, 19 R. des Trois Rois.

Reims.—Engl. Wesleyan Ch., Rue des Moissons, 11 and 6,
and Bd. du Temple.
Ref. Ch., 3, Bd. du Temple, 10.
Bible Dépôt, 7, R. Anquétel.

RENNES.—Protestants 450. Ref. Ch., Bd. de la Liberté, 11.
Bible Dépôt, Desbiot, ruelle du Puits Jacob.
McAll Mission, 111, Rue St. Malo.

Roubaix.—C. and C.C.S., Rev. C. Faulkner ; also at Croix.
Ref. Ch., 41, Rue des Arts, 10.
Flemish Services in Ref. Ch.
McAll Mission, Rue des Fondeurs ; and also at Croix,
Salle de Musique.

Rouen.—C. and C.C.S., All Saints', Rev. S. B. Smyth.
Engl. Wesleyan Ch., 38, Rue Grand Pont, 11 and
6.30, Rev. J. W. Herivel ; private address, 7, Rue
Méridienne, French Evang. Service at 8 p.m.
Protestants, 2,100. Ref. Ch., Place St. Eloi, 10.30.
Fr. Wesleyan Evangelistic Services, 29, Rue Gessand
St. Sever, Friday, 8 p.m.
Seamen's Institute, 38, Rue Grand Pont. Open every
night.
Madame Condurier's Evangelistic Services. Fort-
nightly, Wed., 8 p.m.
McAll Mission, 2 stations : one at Rue de la République,
Sotteville.
Bible Dépôt, 34, Quai de Paris.

Royat-les-Bains. — C. and C.C.S., Engl. Ch., various.
Ref. Ch., in summer, Hôtel Chabassière, 3.

ST. ETIENNE.—Protestants 3,000. Ref. Ch., Rue de la
Paix, 10.45. Free Ch., 9, Rue de la Providence, 11.
Bapt. Ch., 6, Rue du Bas-Vernail.

St. Etienne.

McAll Mission (Director, Dr. Burroughs), 7, Rue de la Banque, and two other *salles.*

Ste. Foy (Gironde).—Protestants 1,700. Ref. Ch., Rue du Temple, 11. Free Ch., Bd. Gratiolet, 11 and 2. *Colonie Agricole* (a Reformatory for boys). Director, Pasteur Thénaud.

St. Hippolyte (Gard).—Protestants 3,600. Ref. Ch. Protestant Establishment for the Deaf, Dumb, and Blind.

St. Jean du Gard.—Protestant pop. 4,000. Ref. Ch., 10.30 ; S. Sch., 2. Free Ch., Rue des Bourgades. Mutual Edification Service, 10.30 ; preaching, 7.30. S. Sch., 1.30.

St. Jean de Luz.—S.P.G. Ch. of Nativity. Rev. J. C. Coen.

St. Malo and St. Servan.—S.P.G. Rev. J. S. Cotton, La Gentillerie, St. Servan.

Eng. Wesleyan Ch., Place du Naye, Gde. Rue, St. Servan, 11. In the Evening at 6.30 ; in *Salle des Conférences,* 7, Rue des Chartres, St. Malo. French services, both at latter place, at 10 and 7.30 ; S. Sch. at 2 p.m. Resident minister, Rev. W. H. Sarchet, 28, Pl. Constantine, St. Servan.

Sailors' Rest (Unsectarian).

St. Martin Lantosque.—S.P.G. July 15 to Aug. 31.

St. Nazaire.

McAll Mission, 9, Rue des Halles.

St. Raphael, Valescure, and Boulérie.—S.P.G. (Nov. to May), Rev. A. F. Dyce.

St. Valéry.—C. and C.C.S.

Saumur.—Ref. Ch., Pl. de la Gendarmerie, 11.15 ; and also at 7.30 in winter ; S. Sch. at 1.

Sedan.—Protestants 1,200. Ref. Ch., Rue des Franc-Bourgeois, 10.30 a.m.

Toulon.—Protestants 1,800. Ref. Ch.

Evangelistic Mission. Director, Pasteur Douèry, 59, Cours Louis Blanc.

TOULOUSE.—Protestants 2,000. Ref. Ch., Rue Romi-
guières, 11.45.
Religious Book Society of Toulouse. Treasurer, M.
Courtois de Viçose, 7, Rue Romiguières.
Asile pour Vieillards et Malades, 57, Allée de la Ré-
publique.
McAll Mission, 105, Grande Rue du Faubourg St
Michel, and two other *salles*.
Tours.—C. and C.C.S. Eng. Ch., Rev. W. Applefor[d].
Protestants 550. Ref. Ch., Rue de la Préfecture,
2 p.m. Bible Dépôt at the Temple.
TREMEL.—Breton Evang. Mission. Pasteur Le Coat.
Services in French and Breton.
Tréport, Le.—C. and C.C.S. Hôt. des Roches Noires.
Trouville.—C. and C.C.S. at Fr. Prot. Ch. July to Sept.
Also French Service in same building on alternate
Sundays.
VALENCE.—Protestants 3,400. Ref. Ch., Rue Sabaterie,
not far from the *Préfecture*, 10.30.
Salvation Army, South-East Division, Major Rabey, 9,
Avenue de Chabeuil. ;
Vichy.—C. and C.C.S. Engl. Ch., various. June to
Sept. Ref. Ch., Place du Marché, 2. Service every
Sunday during the season at 2 o'clock.
VIRE.—Ref. Ch., Place St. Thomas, 10.
N.B.—Reformed doctrines were first preached in
this district in a little chapel on the estate called La
Poupelière. The building still exists. At Athis is a
Protestant Church, built in 1866.

Governesses' and Servants' Homes in France.

PARIS.—106, Faubg. St. Honoré, *Bureau de Renseigne-
ments*, etc.
Home Français, 17, Rue de l'Arc de Triomphe.
Home Suisse, 25, Rue Descombes.
Maison Allemande, 21, Rue Brochant (*Institutrices*).
Maison Allemande, 110, Rue Nollet (*Domestiques*).

PARIS :

Miss Leigh's Home for English Girls, 77, Avenue de Wagram.

Miss Pryde's Institute for Governesses, 162, Rue de Tilsit.

BORDEAUX.—Home Français (*Inst.* and *Domest.*), 9, Rue Mandron.

CANNES.—Maison Hospitalière, apply to Mme. Marrauld, 54, Rue de Fréjus.

LYON.—Bureau de Renseignts., 2, Rue Lafont. Asile pour Domest., 64, Rue Garibaldi.

MARSEILLE.—Œuvre des Servantes, 18, Rue Ste. Victoire.

NICE.—Maison Hospitalière, 22, Rue Siguranne.

In the Track of the Evangelist.

NORTHERN FRANCE.

(1) Land at BOULOGNE, McAll Station, 53, Rue Ad. Thiers. Inquire of Pasteur Dégremont, of Ref. Ch., 54, Bould. Pr. Albert. Pass on to Amiens, from there Doullens and Feuquières, Stations of Soc. Centr., may be reached. Thence to Lille, for Cambrai, Crèvecœur, Maubeuge, and Roubaix ; or to St. Quentin (Pasteur Jean Monnier) for Tergnier, Chauny, Laon, Soissons, Troissy, La Ferté and Paris. This is one of the chief fields of work of Soc. Centr. Secy., Past. Duchemin, 75, R. des Batignolles, Paris.

(2) Land at DIEPPE. Inquire of Pasteur Hardy, R. Jean Ribault. Then to Rouen, Pont-Audemer, Ste. Opportune, Evreux, and Verneuil, all Stations of Soc. Centr., to Chartres and Paris.

(3) Land at CALAIS. Liévin (M. Bion, Evangéliste) ; Hersin-Coupigny (M. Ducros, Pasteur) ; Hersin-Liétard (M. Boyer, Evangéliste). One of the most interesting evangelistic spheres at the present time. Soc. Centrale.

(4) Land at ST. MALO. Wesleyan Mission (see under St. Malo). To Morlaix, Pasteur Jenkins, Bapt. do. ;

NORTHERN FRANCE:

Tremel, Pasteur Le Coat ; Brest, McAll Mission, Pasteur Berthe ; Lorient, Pasteur Kissel ; St. Nazaire and Nantes.

CENTRAL FRANCE.

(1) Paris to Auxerre (Lyons R. to Laroche), Sens, Châtel-Censoir, and Clamecy (Stations of Soc. Ev. de France). Inquire of Past. Mouron, 76, Rue d'Assas, Paris; on to Nevers (Soc. Centr.), Montluçon (Pasteur Seitte's work). Thence to Roanne (Free Ch.), St. Etienne (McAll Mission, Dr. Hastings Burroughs), and Lyons (for work there inquire of Pasteur L. Monod, 5, Rue Sala).

(2) Paris to Orleans. Rail to Limoges, Châteauponsac, for Villefavard (almost wholly Protestant), and Balledent (Stations of Soc. Ev. de France). This district first evangelized by Pasteurs Napoléon Roussel, and L. Pilatte in 1843, etc.

WESTERN FRANCE.

(1) Start from Bordeaux (McAll Mission) to Libourne, Ste. Foy-la-Grande (Free Ch. and *Colonie Agricole*, Pasteur Thénaud ; also St. Aulaye), Bergerac (Free Ch., Pasteur Lemaire), Laforce (John Bost's Asylums), Périgueux (Pasteur Camblong), to Brive (Soc. Ev. de France, Pasteur Crémer).

(2) From Nantes (Pasteur Fargues, 54, Rue de Gigant) to La Roche-s.-Yon (Pasteur Meyer), Pouzauges, Bressuire, Niort (Free Ch. Pasteur, Deschamps, Rue d'Espignole, will give information about work in Saintonge), St. Jean d'Angély, Matha, Saintes (Pasteur Roufineau), Bordeaux.

SOUTHERN FRANCE.

(1) From Lyons (inquire about Htes. Alpes of M. R. de Cazenove, 8, R. Sala, Sec. of Prot. Com. of Lyons)

SOUTHERN FRANCE :
to Grenoble (Pasteur Delavenna, Soc. Ev. Genève),
thence to Htes. Alpes, Felix Neff's region.
(2) From Marseilles (for McAll work, inquire of Pasteur
Em. Lenoir), Montpellier, Béziers, Castres (Pasteur
A. Barnaud, Free Ch.), and Mazamet (Pasteur E.
Barnaud, Free Ch.), Toulouse (Pasteur Vesson),
Montauban (Theol. Faculty of Ref. Ch.).

HINTS FOR TRAVELLERS IN SEARCH OF HUGUENOT MEMORIES.

I.—On the railway from Paris to Tergnier (route
Reims) is Noyon, Calvin's birthplace (1509)—house gone.
The Baptist minister at Chauny has recently begun to
preach here. Further on is St. Quentin, where, in 1557,
Philip II. of Spain, aided by 'bloody Mary,' his wife,
fought against the French under Coligny and Anne de
Montmorency, and defeated them. Philip had vowed
that if successful he would erect a monastery in honour of
his patron, St. Lawrence, who was done to death on a
gridiron. Hence the Escorial Convent in Spain, laid out
as a gridiron.

Still in this region—on the railway from Paris to
Cambrai—is Roisel station. Not far off, in the Valley of
Hesbécourt, is the Boîte à Cailloux, where, after the
Revocation, and almost up to 1789, the pastors of the
Desert preached—among others, Givry, during whose
brief ministry in that region seven churches were
formed.

In three or four hours from Reims, Sedan is reached,
the place of Napoleon's defeat in 1870, but also a spot
famous in the history of the Reformation as the seat of a
Theological Faculty, where the controversialist Pierre
du Moulin taught, and where the pious Drelincourt and
the historian Basnage studied.

II.—At Dieppe the Reformation found an entrance

through a Genevese colporteur, Venable, and John Knox was for a time pastor of the church, which subsequently became so numerous that the members boldly seized the principal church, St. Jacques, and worshipped in it for a whole year.

In 1562, only some twelve months after the *Colloque de Poissy*, Rouen, then held by the Protestants, aided by 500 English, was besieged, and after eleven days fell into the hands of the brutal soldiery of Charles IX. At the present day there are some 2,100 Protestants in and around the city.

Taking train in the direction of Chartres, we come to Buell, ten miles from which is the battle-field of Ivry, where, as Macaulay tells us in his lay, Henri IV. gained so signal a victory over the League in 1590.

At Dreux, the next station, the Duc de Guise routed the Huguenots and took the Prince de Condé prisoner. Above the town are the remains of a castle, which Henri IV. took from the Duc de Guise. Also a chapel, which Louis Philippe built as a burial-place for himself and family. One of the finest sculptures is the work of his daughter.

In the magnificent cathedral at Chartres Henri IV. was crowned in 1594.

Passing thence by rail through the plain of La Beauce in the direction of Brest, we reach Brittany, the eastern part of which was once a stronghold of Protestantism. It was D'Andelot, brother of Admiral Coligny, who introduced Protestantism into Brittany. Taking two preachers with him from Paris they proclaimed the new doctrine at Angers and Nantes. One of their hearers was François de la Noue, who became one of the chief promoters of Breton Protestantism. From Nantes they passed to Blain, where Isabeau de Navarre, the dowager of Rohan received them as 'angels of the Lord.' Thenceforward for many years the Château of Blain was the great Protestant centre, and when Protestantism had been put down in Nantes it was at Blain that the persecuted found a place of refuge. Henri de Rohan, the great Protestant chief, was born at Blain, as also was his distinguished daughter, Anne de Rohan. The château was founded in 1108, and was rebuilt. Two of the towers date from the thirteenth and fourteenth centuries. The greater part of the building is in the Renaissance style. It is reached by the rail from Le Mans towards St. Nazaire (Nantes).

III.—On the railway from Paris to Rouen, and seventeen miles from Paris, is Poissy, the birthplace of St. Louis, and also the town where the memorable but ineffectual conference took place between Romanists and Protestants, shortly after the consecration of Charles IX. at Reims. Théodore de Bèze, assisted by Peter Martyr Vermiglio and others, represented the Protestants at the conference.

IV.—Visitors to the Cathedral of Bourges (railway from Orleans) should remember that Calvin studied law at Bourges, and received his first evangelical impressions there. The neighbouring village of Asnières may be called the cradle of French Protestantism. Between there and Bourges is a bridge still called Calvin's Bridge.

By railway from Bourges to Nevers, and then rail back towards Paris, Châtillon-sur-Loire is reached. The Reformed Church here (Past. Roth) is one of the oldest in France. Châtillon-sur-Loing, further on, near Nogent-sur-Vernis, was the residence of Admiral Coligny.

V.—On the railway from Paris to Strasbourg is the station of Blesme, where a line branches off and traverses the Department of the Haute Marne.

In this region Protestantism once prevailed, especially in the town of Vassy, where so many were massacred by the Duc de Guise in 1562. They were attacked when worshipping in a barn. This building is still in existence, and has been purchased for conversion into a chapel. For many years the Wesleyan Church laboured in this district, but their stations have been handed over to the Reformed Church. The Joinville Château, ' the cradle of the Ducs de Guise,' was not far from Vassy, but was pulled down in 1790.

VI.—The banks of the Loire. Huguenot memories attach to the principal towns. Orleans—once the stronghold of Protestantism—famous for its siege, where Francis, Duke of Guise, was assassinated. This siege ended the first War of Religion. Joan of Arc's name will ever be associated with Orleans.

Blois. In the wonderful Château the Duke of Guise was killed.

Amboise. Noted for the so-called conspiracy, when 1,200 perished, the principal victims being executed as an after-dinner spectacle for the benefit of Catherine de Médicis, Mary Queen of Scots, and her courtiers.

Tours. Near Tours is the colony of Mettray, the well-known Reformatory.

Saumur. Here, for nearly four months, the representatives of the Protestants (from fifteen provinces) met under the presidency of Duplessis Mornay, trying to secure their rights. Here, too, was the famous Protestant Academy (founded in 1617), the teaching at which was a sort of transition from Calvinism to Arminianism. Moïse Amyraut was one of its ablest professors. Students flocked hither from England, Scotland and Germany. Under Duplessis Mornay, who was appointed governor, the town became an important one of 25,000 inhabitants ; but at the Revocation of the Edict of Nantes the Huguenots were driven away, and only about 6,000 people remained.

Angers. The Reformed Church building dates from the twelfth century.

Nantes. Memorable for the Edict which gave a certain amount of freedom to the Protestants, and the Revocation of which well-nigh ruined France.

VII.—From Tours, Poitiers is reached by rail in two or three hours. It was between Poitiers and Tours that Chas. Martel defeated the Saracenic host in 732, and thus stayed the great Mahometan invasion. At Poitiers, Calvin laboured in the early part of his career. Near the town is the cave of St. Bénoit, called Calvin's Grotto, where Calvin opened his mind fully to a number of thoughtful, cultured men, and then asked them to join him in prayer. According to Florimel de Reymond, he prayed with much vehemence.

The old provinces of the Poitou and the Saintonge were greatly stirred by the Reformation movement. It is recorded that thirty-three temples in the Poitou were destroyed by Louis XIV., in 1665. At the present day, Protestantism is largely represented there, and is beginning to show some signs of life.

By rail from Poitiers to Loudun (first Protestant Synod held here in 1555) and Chantonnay, and from thence by diligence (7½ miles) Mouchamp is reached. Just north of this, on the confines of a vast forest, are the remains of the Château de Parc-Soubise, where the famous Catherine de Parthenay spent her youth. She married Viscount René de Rohan, at La Rochelle, in 1575, and was the mother of Anne de Rohan, born at Blain in 1584. (See *Derniers Récits du 16me Siècle,* par Jules Bonnet.)

From Poitiers direct by rail to La Rochelle, once the great Protestant stronghold, the siege of which is the most thrilling story in French Protestant history. It began in 1627, and lasted more than a year, the English three times making a show of coming to the help of the starving people, but eventually failing to do so. Before this, in 1568, Condé, Coligny, and D'Andelot took refuge here, and were joined by Jeanne d'Albret, Queen of Navarre, and by the chief Huguenot leaders from Normandy, Maine, and Anjou. Then began the third War of Religion.

A Protestant church was first formed in 1558. For some years Protestants and Catholics lived on good terms, and used the churches of St. Sauveur and St. Barthélemy in common. Here the Synod was held under the presidency of Theod. de Bèze, at which the confession of faith and discipline was revised and adopted as the symbol of the Reformed Church of France.

VIII.—Béarn, the present department of the *Basses Pyrénées*, is full of Protestant memories. Marguerite de Valois, mother of Jeanne d'Albret, took refuge here. Under Jeanne's influence Béarn became a most moral province. Schools and hospitals were established, and a new code of laws framed. She was the noble mother of Henri IV., who proved himself an unworthy son. The ruins of Jeanne's château are still to be seen at Bellocq, near Puyoo, on line from Dax to Pau.

At Bayonne, Catherine de Médicis had a conference with the Duke of Alva, in 1565 ; and together they agreed, it is said, on the massacre of St. Bartholomew.

Orthez, also on line from Dax to Pau. The church here was the most important of those in Béarn in the early days of Protestantism. Jeanne d'Albret founded a Protestant Academy here in 1566. It was destroyed in 1620. At that period the church had four pastors, three of whom were also professors at the Academy. There were then thirty Protestant temples in that district. From 1822 to 1830 a remarkable revival took place in Béarn, in connection with the labours of Henri Pyt, agent of the Continental Society of London. At present there is a Reformed Church at Orthez, and also a Free Church.

IX.—The Cévennes. This mountainous region— still mainly Protestant—abounds in historic memories. Here the Camisards fought for their liberties, but in vain. The traveller who is determined to penetrate into it must not expect to find hotels or even decent inns. Headquarters may be taken up at Anduze, just outside the great natural gate by which the region is entered on that side. Anduze is reached by rail from Nîmes. In a barn at Bagard, Cavalier held his first meeting and formed his band of Camisards. St. Jean du Gard is the chief town of this part of the Cévennes (Reformed Church, Pasteur Meinadier ; Free Church, Pasteur Guibal), and not far distant is Mialet (Reformed Church, Pasteur Chasland)— the country of the two Camisard chiefs, the Laportes. Close by is Massoubeyran, birthplace of Roland Laporte, whose hiding-place beneath the kitchen-floor in an old house is still to be seen ; also his Bible and *hallebardes*. Near by are caves which served as arsenals.

X.—Nîmes is rich in Protestant associations as well as Roman remains. The Grand Temple was hired in 1792, and after 106 years' cessation, Protestant worship was recommenced, the Patriarch of the Desert, Paul Rabaut, offering the dedicatory prayer. At the *Orphelinat* (for information ask Pasteur Dardier, 1, Rue Trajan) is Pasteur Rabaut's tomb. In a corner of the Protestant cemetery is a small building used as a vestry by the pastors of the Desert when they preached at the *Ermitage*.

A deeply interesting excursion from Nîmes by rail to Aiguesmortes. Train passes through 'the little Canaan' as it was called, because so largely a Protestant district in former days. Aiguesmortes is a town fortified by St. Louis, after the manner of Jerusalem, and the fortifications are all perfect. Just outside the walls is the Tower of Constance, where Huguenot prisoners—notably Marie Durand—were held captive for long years.

BELGIUM.
Population in 1887, 5,974,743.

There are eleven Reformed Churches in Belgium supported by the State, viz., Antwerp, Brussels (2), Dour, Ghent, Liège, Maria-Hoorebeek, Pâturages, Seraing, Tournay, Verviers. The churches of Dour, Maria-Hoorebeek, and Rongy-Tournay date from the time of the Reformation.

The Reformed Church has an Evangelization Committee which supports stations at Cuesme, Douvrain, La Louvière, Leuze, Malines, Roulers, and Wasme.

Christian Missionary Church or Evangelical Society. Secretary, M. le Pasteur Kennedy Anet, 32, Rue Tasson-Snel, Brussels. Office of the Society, 123, Chaussée d'Ixelles, Brussels.

The Belgian Christian Missionary Church has churches
and stations at Antwerp, Boussu, Brussels (2), Charleroi,
Chênée, Clabecq, Courcelles, Frameries, Ghent, Jumet,
La Louvière, La Roche, Court—St. Etienne, Liège, Lize—
Seraing, Morville, Namur, Nessonvaux, Ostend, Paifve,
Quaregnon, Sart-Dame-Avelines, Spa, Sprimont, Tain-
tegnies, Verviers, Wasme. In all, twenty-eight churches
and stations ; also fourteen colporteurs.

Antwerp.—Engl. Episc. Ch., C. and C.C.S., 23, Rue des
Tanneurs, 11 and 7. Rev. A. Pryde, 34, Rue Monte-
bello. Mariners' Ch. and Inst., 21, Avenue du Com-
merce, 11 and 7. Chaplain, Mr. J. Hitchens.
Ref. Ch., 5, Longue Rue de la Boutique. Flemish
Service, 9.30 and 5 ; and German, 11.
Scandinavian Lutheran Ch., 8, Avenue du Commerce.
German, 12 ; and Norwegian, 10 and 6.
Chr. Miss. Ch., 3, Rue de l'Ecuelle. Flemish, 10 and 5.
Bible Dépôts, Stynders, 9, Elisabeth Straat, and at the
Mariners' Institute.
Blankenberghe.—S.P.G., R. Breydel, July 15 to Sept. 15.
Bruges.—Engl. Episc. Ch., Rue d'Ostende, 11 and 7
(winter 5.30). Rev. A. V. Hughes-Hallett, 30, Rue
du Vieux Sac.
Brussels.—Engl. Episc. Ch. (1) Church of the Resur-
rection, Rue de Stassart, 8.30, 11, 3.45, and 7. Rev.
J. C. Jenkins, 74, Rue de Stassart.
(2) 13, Rue Belliard, 8.30, 12, and 4. Rev. A. K. Har-
lock, 60, Rue de la Longue Haie.
(3) Rue Crespel, Avenue de la Toison d'Or (C. and
C.C.S.), 11 and 7 (in summer 7.45). Rev. W. R.
Stephens, 171, Chaussée de Vleurgat.
Ref. Ch. (1) Chapelle du Musée (Chapelle Royale),
German service, 10.30 ; French do., 12.
(2) 5, Pl. Ste. Catherine. Flemish Service, 10.30 and 5.
Ch. Miss. Ch., 13, Rue Belliard, 10.30 and 6. Flemish
services, 93, Rue Blaes.
French Wesleyan Ch., 49, Bd. Bischoffsheim, 11 and

Salles d'Evangélisation :

(1) French Meetings, directed by Pasteur Meyhoffer (85, Rue Mercelis, private address).

Rue du Métal, 49. Wednesday, 8 p.m. S. Sch., 3. French.

Rue Goffart, 49. Friday, 8 p.m. S. Sch., 3. French.

(2) Flemish Meetings, directed by Pasteur Hacksteen. 93, Rue Blaes, Sunday, 8 p.m.

Molenbeek St. Jean, 75, Rue Ransfort. Tuesday and Friday, 8 p.m., and Sunday, 2 p.m.

(3) Directed by Pasteur De Jonge (344, Rue des Palais, private address).

Silo, 311, Chaussée d'Anvers.

Peniel, 209, Chaussée de Mons. Meetings every evening at 8, except Saturdays, in Flemish.

Book, Bible, and Tract Dépôt, 123, Chaussée d'Ixelles.

B. and F. Bible Society's Agency, Mr. W. H. Kirkpatrick, 5, Rue de la Pépinière.

Y.M.C.A., 9, Pl. Ste. Catherine.

Institute for English Governesses and Servants, 26, Rue de Vienne. Free, and open daily till 9.30 p.m.

Prot. Orphanage, 147, Chaussée d'Alsemberg, Uccle.

Prot. Hospital, 338, Chaussée de Wavre.

CHARLEROI.—Chr. Miss. Ch., New Chapel, Bd. Central, 10 a.m.

Courtrai.—United British Prot. Ch., 96, Faubourg de Gand, 11.30, 3, and 6.30.

Ref. Ch., Flemish in same place, 9.30.

Ghent, or Gand —S.P.G., Place St. Jacques, 11 and 7.

Rev. C. F. Mermagen, 8, Quai des Tanneurs.

Ref. Ch., Rue Digue de Brabant. Flemish, 9.30.

Chr. Miss. Ch., 25, Bd. Grand Béguinage. Flemish, 10 and 4.

LIÈGE.—Ref. Ch., Rue Hors Château. French, 10 a.m.

Chr. Miss. Ch., 12, Rue Lambert-le-Bègue. French, 10 and 6.

NAMUR.—Chr. Miss. Ch., 9, Place Léopold, 10.

Ostend.—S.P.G., Rue Longue, 8.30, 11, 3.30, and 7. Rev.
L. M. D'Orsey.
Chr. Miss. Ch., 46, Albertustraat. Flemish.

Spa.—S.P.G., Rev. J. Harrison, 8.30 and 11.30. Presb.
Ch., Rue Brixhe, in July and August, 4 p.m.
Chr. Miss. Ch., Rue Brixhe, 10 and 7 p.m.

TOURNAI.—Ref. Ch., 10.

VERVIERS.—Ref. Ch., Rue Saucy. Chr. Miss. Ch., Rue
Donkier, 11 and 7.

EVANGELISTIC WORK IN BELGIUM.

Good work is being done in Brussels under the direction of (1) Pasteur de Jonge and (2) Pasteurs Meyhoffer
and Haksteen. See under *Brussels.*

The mining district of Charleroi is also interesting in
this respect — chapels at Charleroi, Jumet, and La
Louvière. Inquire of Past. Anet, 123, Chaussée d'Ixelles,
Brussels.

Mission Sunday Schools for children of Roman
Catholics are to be found in Brussels and in the
mining districts, and, though small, are interesting and
most useful. In all, 20 of these schools.

HOLLAND.

Population in 1887, 4,450,870. In 1879—Protestants,
2,469,814 ; Rom. Catholics, 1,445,425 ; Jews, 81,693.

Protestant Churches paid by the State : 1. Netherlands
Ref. Ch. ; Universities, Utrecht, Groningen, Leyden
and Amsterdam (Free University, Ultra-Calvinistic).
2. Evangl. Lutheran Ch. ; Theological Seminary at
Amsterdam. 3. Restored Evangl. Luth. Ch. 4.¹
Remonstrant Ch. ; Theological Seminary at Leyden.
5. Walloon Ch.

Free Churches : 1. Christian Dissenting Ref. Ch., estab.
1834, about 380 communities and 150,000 members ;
Theol. Sch. at Kampen. 2. Mennonite Chs., 127 ;

Theol. Seminary at Amsterdam. 3. Moravians, 2 · chs. 4. In 1886 a church was organized on basis of Confession of 1618, by a body of separatists from Ref. Est. Ch. 5. Baptists, 3 chapels, 157 members. 6. Dutch Baptist Union, 17 chs., 996 members, and 1,184 S. scholars.

The principal Sunday Service at most Dutch chs. begins at 10 a.m.

Dutch Missions to the Heathen : ·

1. Netherlands Miss. Soc. (1797). Director of Mission House, J. C. Neurdenburg, Rotterdam. Sphere, East Indies.
2. Netherlands Miss. Union (1858). Director, S. Coolsma, Rotterdam. Sphere, West Java.
3. Utrecht Miss. Union (1859). Director, Dr. A. A. Looyen. Sphere, New Guinea.
4. Mission of the Christian Ref. Ch. in the Netherlands. Director, J. H. Donner, Leyden. Sphere, Batavia.
5. Amsterdam Java Committee. President, Mr. T. M. Looman. Sphere, Java, Sumatra, Madoera.
6. Bapt. Miss. Soc. (1847). Sphere, Java, Sumatra.
7. Moravian Miss. (1798). Sphere, Surinam, Labrador, etc.
8. Ermelo Miss. Soc. (1846). Sphere, Java and Egypt.

Arnheim.—C. and C.C.S.

B. and F. Bible Soc. Dépôt, Mr. H. B. Breyer. Deaconesses' Institute.

Rev. C. Ad. v. Scheltema, editor of various evangelical publications.

Amsterdam.—C. and C.C.S. Engl. Episc. Ch., Rev. J. Chambers. Presb. Ch., Bagynenhof.

Walloon Ch., Walepleintje ; also at 276, Keizersgracht, 10.

Salvation Army—Headquarters, 44, Rapenberg, and 21 other places in Holland.

B. and F. Bible Soc. Dépôt, Mr. H. G. Bom, Warmoestraat.

AMSTERDAM :
Free Church of Scotland Mission to Jews. Services conducted by agents of the Netherlands Society for Israel.
Netherlands Bible Society Dépôt, Warmoesstraat, 149.
London Jews' Society. Rev. A. C. Adler, 229, O.Z. Achterburgwal.
Rel. Tr. Society Publications. Höveker and Son, Heerengracht, by Wolvestraat.
Sunday School Union, Bloemgracht, 79. Secretary, Mr. T. M. Looman, M. J. Kosterstraat, 12.
Temperance Coffee Houses : 'De Hoop,' de Ruyter-kade.
Patrimonium, or Chr. Assn. for Workmen, with branches all over the land (1881). President, K. Kater, Utrecht.

DOETICHEM.—Schools for Training Young Men for the Ministry.
B. and F. Bible Soc., Rev. Van Dijk.

GRONINGEN.—Miss de Ranitz' Christian Institute.
B. and F. Bible Soc., Mr. W. Ornée.

Hague.—C. and C.C.S., St. John and St. Philip. Rev. E. Brine. Walloon Ch., Nordende, 10 and 2.
B. and F. Bible Soc., Mr. L. Voorneveld, Molenstr.
Deaconesses' Institute.

KAMPEN.—Theol. Sch. of Free Ch. Profs. Dr. Bavink, L. Lindenboom, and Wielengach.
B. and F. Bible Soc., Mr. G. F. Zalsman.

LEIDEN.—Salvation Army, 17, Werffstraat.
B. and F. Bible Soc. Dépôt, Mr. K. de Geus, Hooigracht.

NEERBOSCH, near Nymegen.—Orphanage with 600 children. Director, M. van t'Lindenhout.

NYMEGEN. — Evangl. Books and Tracts, Mr. P. T. Milborn.
Deaconesses' Establishment.
B. and F. Bible Soc., Mr. P. T. Milborn.

Rotterdam.—Engl. Episc. Ch., C. and.C.C.S., St. Mary's, Haringvliet, 11 a.m., Rev. J. Attridge.

Presb. Ch., Vasteland, 10.30 and 6.30.

Walloon Ref. Ch. (French), 398, Hoogstr., 10.

Y.M.C.A., Obadja Jonker Fraustr.

B. and F. Bible Soc., Mr. W. Wenk, Blaak, and Mr. J. M. Bredée, Molenstraat.

B. and F. Sailors' Soc. Institute, 113, Boompjes, Mr. J. Jones. Bethel Services, English, Sunday evening, 7 ; Mondays and Fridays, 7.30.

Blind Asylum, Kruiskade.

Deaf and Dumb Asylum, Coolsingel.

Tract Dépôt, Mr. Herklots, 46, Boompjes.

Mission House in Rechter—Rottekade, Museum always open.

UTRECHT. Walloon Ch.

Salvation Army, Weistraat.

B. and F. Bible Soc. Head Dépôt, Pausdam, F. 274 ; agent, Mr. H. Grelinger.

Deaconesses' Establishment.

ZETTEN. — Talitha Kumi, Bethel, Magdalen Asylum, Steenbeek.

ZEIST, near Utrecht.—Moravian Colony. Bethanië.

ZWOLLE.—B. and F. Bible Soc., Mr. Tulp.

GERMANY.

THE EMPIRE.—Population in 1885, 46,855,704. Protestants, 28,330,967 ; R. Catholics, 16,232,606 ; Jews 561,612.

PRUSSIA.—Population in 1885, 28,318,470. Protestants, 18,244,405 ; R. Catholics, 9,621,763 ; Jews, 366,575.

SAXONY.—Population in 1885, 3,182,003. Protestants, 3,075,654 ; R. Catholics, 86,952 ; Jews, 7,755.

WURTEMBERG.—Population in 1885, 1,995,185. Protestants, 1,377,805 ; R. Catholics, 598,223 ; Jews, 13,171.

BADEN.—Population in 1885, 1,601,255. Protestants, 565,236 ; R. Catholics, 1,004,276 ; Jews, 27,104.

ALSACE-LORRAINE.—Population in 1885, 1,564,355. Protestants, 312,941 ; R. Catholics, 1,210,297 ; Jews, 36,876.

BAVARIA.—Population in 1885, 5,420,199.

Protestant Churches:
1. Evangl. Ch.—Union of Reformed and Lutheran.
2. Lutheran Ch.
3. German Bapt. Union. Associations, 6 ; churches, 102 ; preaching stations, 828 ; chapels, 84 ; S. scholars, 14,659 ; and members, 19,009.
4. Episcopal Meth. Ch. Mission. 5 Districts. 1, Berlin, District Elder, H. Mann, Leipzig. 2, Bremen, Elder, F. Klüsner, Oldenburg. 3, Frankfort, Elder, A. Sulzberger, 88, Röderberg, Frankfurt-am-M. 4, Karlsruhe, Elder, C. Gebhardt, Karlsruhe. 5, Würtemberg, Elder J. Staeger, Heilbronn. 59 native ordained preachers, 7,296 members, and 10,723 S. scholars. Publishes 6 periodicals. Book Steward, Rev. H. Nuelsen, 59, Georgstr., Bremen.
5. Wesleyan Meth. Ch. 26 missionaries ; 23 chapels ; 197 other preaching places ; 2,397 members ; and 3,233 S. scholars. Supt., Rev. J. C. Barratt, Cannstatt, nr. Stuttgart.

The principal Sunday Service in the Protestant State Chs. begins at 9.30 or 10 a.m.

The B. and F. Society's Editions of German Bibles, etc., may be had through almost any bookseller.

Kingdom of Würtemberg :
The Protestant Church is called Evangelical, and is Lutheran in doctrine, though its form of service resembles that of the Reformed (Calvinist) Ch. Divided into 6 districts, at the head of each of which is a General Superintendent, and into 49 Dioceses, directed by Superintendents or Deans (*Dekan*) ; 1,026 Pastors.

The form of religious life characteristic of Würtemberg and the means of maintaining *Pietism* is the *Gebetstunde*, a fraternal gathering for reading of the Scriptures and mutual edification. It is reckoned that as many as 70,000 persons regularly attend these meetings.

There is a Training School for Home Missionaries at Karlshöhe, near Ludwigsburg.

Dr. A. H. Werner's Infirmaries at Ludwigsburg, Jagstfeld, and Wildbad.

The late G. Werner's Philanthropic Institutions at Reutlingen and other places.

Arbeiterkolonieen (Workmen's Colonies), at Domahof and other places.

The most celebrated preachers of Würtemberg are Dr. Gerok, Dr. Burk, Dekan Weitbrecht, and Dr. Braun, all in Stuttgart, and Dr. Kuebel in Tübingen.

Missions to the Heathen :

(1) Rhenish Miss. Soc.—Inspector, Dr. A. Schreiber, Barmen, Mission House. (South Africa, Borneo, Sumatra, and China.)

(2) Berlin Soc.—Director, Rev. Dr. Merensky, Berlin. (S. Africa.)

(3) Moravian Miss. Soc.—Secretary, Bishop Kühn, Berthelsdorf, near Herrnhut, Saxony. (Africa and West Indies.)

(4) Gossner Miss., or Evangl. Miss. Soc.—Director, Prof. Plath, Berlin. (Amongst the Kols.)

(5) North German Mission.—Inspector Zahn, Bremen. (West Africa, among the Ewes.)

(6) Leipzig Lutheran Mission.—Director, Dr. Hardeland, Leipzig. (Tamil country, India.)

(7) Hermannsburg Mission (the late Pastor Harms).— Secretary, Rev. Harms, Hermannsburg, Hanover. (S. Africa chiefly ; also Australia, and Telugu country, India.)

(8) Brecklum, Schleswig, Lutheran Miss. Seminary.

(9) Ladies' Soc. for the Orient.—Secretary, Mr. Marwart, 4, Friedensstrasse, Berlin.

(10) Bâle Miss. Soc.—Inspector Oehler, Basel. (East Indies, Africa, China.)

(11) East African Mission.—Inspector, D. C. G. Buttner 10, Weimbergsweg, Berlin, N.

(12) St. Crischona, a Pilgrim Miss.—Director Haarbeck, Crischona, near Bâle. (Sends out labourers to all parts.)

Aix la Chapelle (Aachen).—S.P.G., Anna-str., Rev. W. C. Bell.

ALTONA.—Bapt. Ch. (German), 98, Grosse Gärtnerstr., 9 and 5.

Baden-Baden.—S.P.G., All Saints', Rev. T. A. S. White B. and F. Bible Society's Stand—open June to Sept.

BAD BOLL, near Göppingen.—Pastor Blumhardt's Faith Healing place.

Badenweiler.—C. and C.C.S., The Belvedere.

BARMEN.—Missionshaus. Evangelisches Vereinshaus,* 10, Bahnhofstr. Bapt. Ch. (German), 44, Gass-str. Religious Tract Society's publications to be had of Wupperthal Tract Society, 33, Wertherstr.

Berlin.—Eng. Ep. Ch. Episc. Meth. Ch., 6, Junkerstr., S.W. American and English Union Service at 11.30. In German at 9.30 and 6.

Bapt. Ch. (German), 17, Schmidtstr., S.O., 9.30 and 4.

Moravian Ch., 136, Wilhelmstr.

French Ch., 26, Gensdarmenmarkt. Services at 10 and 3 alternately in summer, and 6 in winter.

City Mission (30 agents), President, Hofprediger Stöcker.

Evangl. Mission, by Mr. J. Rohrbach, 8, Bremerstr., Moabit, N.W. Also at Charlottenburg.

B. and F. Bible Society, Mr. J. Watt, Agent, 33, Wilhelmstr., S.W.

---

* The *Vereinshaus* is the headquarters of the Y.M.C.A. Bed and board may be had.

BERLIN :

London Jews' Society, Rev. Prof. Cassel, D.D., Gross-beererstr., 96, II.

German Book and Tract Soc., 142, Ackerstr., Secretary, Baron v. Ungern Sternberg.

Religious Tract Society's Dépôt, Mr. E. Beck, 142, Ackerstr., N. Also at 29, Behrenstr., W.

City Mission Hotel (good), Hospiz der Stadtmission, 27, Mohrenstr., W.

Christlicher Verein junger Männer, 34, Wilhelmstr.

Y.M.C.A. and Vereinshaus, 106, Oranienstr.

New Vereinshaus (of a superior order), 'Friedefürst,' Weddingplatz, N.

Vereinshaus, 29, Behrenstr., near Central Hotel. Daily Prayer Meeting at 12.30.

Gossner Mission-house, 131, Potsdamerstr.

Berlin Miss. Soc. for Africa, Rev. Dr. Merensky, 5, Friedenstr., N.O.

Cabmen's Mission, Mrs. Palmer Davies, *née* Freiinn von Dungern, 135, Alt Moabit.

Evang. Johannestift on the Plötzensee, including a Brüderhaus for training men to attend on prisoners, sick, poor, etc.

BIELEFELD.—Deaconesses' Institute, 'Sarepta.' Home for Epileptics. Bethel—first German workmen's colony (3 hours from Bielefeld), founded by Pastor von Bodelschwingh.

Bonn.—Engl. Episc. Ch. (in University Church).

Presb. Services occasionally in the Johanneum in the summer.

Johanneum, 30, Lennestr., Training School for Evangelists in connection with German Evangelization Socy. President, Rev. Prof. Christlieb, D.D., University Preacher. Prayer Meetings, Wednesday and Friday. S. School—the oldest in Germany.

Boppart.—S.P.G. July 15 to Aug. 31.

BREMEN.—Population in 1885, 165,628. Meth. Episc. Ch., 59, Georgstr., 9.30 and 5.

BREMEN :

Inner Mission. Treasurer, J. Volckmann, 16, Bornstr.

Y.M.C.A. Vereinshaus, 6, Ansgarii, Kirchhof.

Bapt. Ch., 115, Langenstr.

Moravian Ch., 7, Ansgarii, Kirchhof.

Temperance (not abstinence) Society. Director, A. Lammers, 128, Humboldtstr.

Pastors Funcke and Tiesmeyer, friends of Home Mission and Sunday Schools.

Rel. Tr. Society's publications at Meth. Ep. Bookstore, 59, Georgstr.

Herbergen zur Heimath, Ansgarii, Kirchhof, 6, and Langenstr., Oldenburger Haus.

People's Circulating Libraries, Supt. Dr. D. A. Noltenius, Humboldtstr., 162.

S. Schools in connection with all Evangelical Churches.

Care for Emigrants, Pastor Cuntz, Rolandstr., 1.

Temperance Coffee Houses, Langenstr. and Nordstr.

BREMERHAVEN.—Meth. Episc. Ch., 21a, Fähstr., 9.30 and 5. Bapt., 11, Geustr., Lehe.

BRESLAU.—Free Evangelical Ch., Free Ch. of Scotland, Jews' Society, 5a, Zwingerstr., 10 and 5 in German, and S. Sch. at 8.45 a.m. Rev. D. Edward, 1, Claassenstr.

London Jews' Soc., Rev. W. Becker, 3f, Brüderstr.

Brit. Jews' Soc., Rev. F. Dworkowicz, Alexanderstr., 5 II.

Deaconesses' Institute, 'Bethanien,' 171 Sisters.

Y.M.C.A., Zwingerstr. 5a.

Tract Dépôt, 92, Friedrichstr.

Bible Dépôt, M. A. Rudolph, 7, Neumarkt.

CALW.—Meth. Episc. Ch., 9.30 and 5. Book Soc., Calwer Buch-Verein.

CANNSTATT.—Wesl. Ch., Karls-str., 9.30 and 7.30.

'Faith-Healing,' Villa Seckendorf (Fräulein A. Schlichter), Olgastr., 124.

Supt. of Germ. Wesl. Mission, Rev. J. C. Barratt, 15, Carlsstr.

Carlsruhe.—S.P.G. Diakonissen-haus Chapel, Rev. L.
A. Wynne. City Mission.
Meth. Episc. Ch., 9.30 and 5. Pastor's address, 22,
Karl Friedrichstr.

Cassel.—C. and C.C.S. St. Alban's, Rev. E. J. Robin-
son. Meth. Episc. Ch., 9, Hollandischstr. Bapt.
Ch., 10, Mönchbergstr.

Cleve.—C. and C.C.S., at Bad Hotel.

Coblenz.—C. and C.C.S. Chapel in Palace.

Cologne.—S.P.G. 3, Bischofsgartenstr., Rev. R. Skinner.
Un. Amer. Ep. Ch., 11. Bapt. Ch. (German), 8,
Rheingasse. B. and F. Bible Soc., 22, Komödienstr.

Constance.—C. and C.C.S. Constanzer Hof. Various.

DANZIG.—Moravian Ch., Johannisgasse, 6 p.m. Bapt.
Ch., 13, Schiesstange, 9.30 a.m.
London Jews' Soc., Herr C. Urbachat, 32, Langgarten.
Deaconesses' Institute, Neugarten, 80-90 Sisters.

Darmstadt.—Engl. Episc. Ch. Deaconesses' Institute
(Elisabethenstift), 69 Sisters.

Dresden.—Engl. Episc. Ch., Wienerstr., 11 and 6. Est.
Ch. of Scotland, Winkelmanstr., 11, Rev. J. D.
Bowden. Amer. Episc. Ch., Bergstr., 11.
Brit. Jews' Soc., Rev. G. F. Schwartz, 10, Mathildenstr.
Rel. Tract Society's publications, Mr. Otto Finger, Neu
Striesen.

Düsseldorf.— C. and C.C.S. Bergenstr., Rev. W. J.
Drought.

Elberfeld and Barmen and the Wupperthal form the
headquarters of many religious and philanthropic
institutions. The Wupperthal Festival Week is the
second week in August.
Engl. Ch. Service (C. and C.C.S.), on Sunday, at 6.30,
in Gemeindehaus at Elberfeld.
Evang. Books and Tracts, Mr. R. Blanch, 10, Gustavstr.
B. and F. Bible Society. Bible House of Berg. Bible
Society.

Ems.—S.P.G., June to Sept. Bible Stand in summer
near Kurhaus.

FLENSBURG (Schleswig).—Meth. Episc. Ch., 817, Holm, 9.30 and 5.

Frankfort (Frankfurt-am-Main).—Population 160,000, of whom 15,000 Jews. S.P.G. 7, Goetheplatz, Rev. G. W. Mackenzie, 11.15 and 3.30. Egl. Ref. Française, 7, Goetheplatz, 9.30. Eight Lutheran churches and twelve pastors. Episc. Meth. Ch. (German), Kornmarkt, 9.30 and 5. Bapt. Ch., 100, Rooenstr. Y.M.C.A., Rheinische Hof, Buchgasse. Also a Y.M.C.A., at 4, Seumenstr., has a S. School at the Marianplatz, about 700 children. B. and F. Bible Soc., Mr. J. Watt, agent, 17, Hochstr. London Jews' Soc., Rev. A. Bernstein, 122, Oederweg. Episc. Meth. Missionary College, Röderberg.

Freiburg im Breisgau.—S.P.G. 51, Kaiserstr., Rev. G. J. Banner.

GERNSBACH.—Centre of Publications of Baden Colportage Soc., Director Baron Julius v. Gemmingen.

GNADENFELD (Upp. Silesia). —Moravian Settlement and Theological Seminary. Director,'Rev. Dr. Plitt.

Gotha.—S.P.G., at Innungshalle, Rev. O. T. H. Flex.

Hamburg.—Population in 1885, 518,620 ; Prots. 477,937, R. Cath. 15,399, Jews 16,848. Engl. Episc. Ch., Zeughausmarkt, 11 a.m., Rev. C. F. Weidemann, Allée, 241, Altona (private address). Engl. Cong. Ch., Johannes Bollwerk, 11 and 6, Rev. J. Atkinson, Wohlers Allée, 42, Altona (private address). Sailors' Institute (Brit. and For. Sailors' Soc.), 3, Brookthor Quay, service on Sunday at 7 p.m. Missionary, Mr. J. C. Jones.

Services at the National Prot. Chs. (German), at 9.30 and 1 p.m.

Bapt. Chap. (German), 21, Böhmkenstr., 9 and 5; also at Hamm, 98, Bostelmannsweg, 9.30 and 5.

Bapt. Theol. Seminary, Rennbahnstr., Hamm. President, Rev. Dr. Bickel, Profs. Lehmann and Fetzer ; 19 students.

HAMBURG :

Bapt. Publication Soc., Bergfelde, 98, Mittelweg.

Director, Rev. Dr. Bickel (*Wahrheitszeuge*, official organ of denomination).

Meth. Episc. Ch. (German), Kleine Kirchenweg, 10, St. Georg, 10 and 5.

Rauhe Haus, Horn—Reformatory, etc., founded by the late Dr. Wichern; also headquarters of Inner Mission, embracing various departments of Evangelical agency.

Town Mission—21 agents and 2 Herbergen zur Heimath (Christian Inns for Workmen), 4, Zimmerstr., Klosterthor, and 3, Hopfenstr., St. Pauli. Secretary, Baron von Oertzen, 1, Ansgarplatz.

London Jews' Soc., Rev. S. T. Bachert, Bären Allée, 6, Wandsbeck.

British Jews' Soc., Mr. G. Neumann, Carolinenstr., 3, II., 2, St. Pauli.

Lower Saxony Tract Soc. Dépôt, Brennerstr., 51.

Jews' Miss. of the Irish Presb. Ch., Königstr., Rev. M. Aston, Waterloostr., 7, Altona (private address).

Deaconesses' Hospitals, St. Ansgarplatz and Bethesda, St. Georg, Burgstr.

Bible Dépôt at the Rauhe Haus Bookshop.

Hanover.—Amer. Episc. Ch.

Bapt. Ch. (German), 10, Semenerstr.

B. and F. Bible Society's Dépôt, Schmorl u. von Seefeld's Buchhandlung.

Deaconesses' Institution (Henriettenstift), 135 Sisters.

Stephanstift.—Reformatory and Hospital for Sick Men.

Heidelberg.—S.P.G. Plöckstr., Rev. S. Hall.

Germ. Evangelical services in Past. Frommels' Ch.

HEILBRONN.—Meth. Episc. Ch., 40, Ausserer Rosenberg, 9.30 and 5. Bapt. Ch., 30, Herbststr.

HERMANNSBURG.—Mission House, Pastor Harms.

HERRNHUT.—The Central Moravian Settlement.

Homburg.—C. and C.C.S. Engl. Ch., Rev. G. B. Brigstocke. Est. Ch. Scotland (in summer). Bible Stand in the Park.

KIEL.—Bapt. Ch., 4, Teichstr.

Meth. Ep. Ch., Pastor's address, 33, Annenstr.

Kissingen.—C. and C.C.S. All Saints', May to Sept.

KÖNIGSBERG. — British Jews' Soc., Prediger Jacobi, Hospital Kirche, Hinter Vorstadt.

Deaconesses' Institution, 126 Sisters.

KORNTHAL (Würtemberg).—Christian Settlement.

Kreuznach.—C. and C.C.S., St. Paul's. (May to Sept.)

LIEGNITZ (Silesia).—Colportage Work. Director, Pastor Streez.

Leipzig.—United Brit. and Amer. Episc. Ch. S.P.G. All Saints, Seb. Bachstr., Rev. J. B. Hardinge. Amer. Ch., Erste Bürgerschule, 5 p.m.

Bapt. Ch., 7, Conradstr., Volkmersdorf.

Mission House, Dr. Hardelande, 19, Carolinenstr., Centre of Luth. Miss. Soc. and Seminary.

B. and F. Bible Soc. and Publisher of Rel. Literature, Justus Naumann, 7, Königstr.

Vereinshaus (Centre of Home Mission Work). Director, Rev. Zinsser, 14, Ross-str. Pr. Meeting, Saturday Evg., 7. Also under same roof Evangl. Hospiz (Christian Hotel of superior order). Also bookshop for sale of Bibles, etc.

Institutum Judaicum, 4, Johannisgasse. Students' Mission to the Jews. Missionary, W. Faber.

Martinsstift, 51, Arndtstr. (Bg. Sch. for Girls in moral danger).

Deaconesses' Institution, 31, Carolinenstr.

Herberge zur Heimath, 21, Ulrichgasse.

Herberge für Dienstmädchen, 19, Kolgartenstr. (for Maid-servants).

MAYENCE.—Bapt. Ch., 14, Lothbarstr.

Memel.—C. and C.C.S. Engl. Ch., R. W. Price. Bapt. Ch., 1, Neuer Park.

MULHOUSE (Mühlhausen).—Bapt. Ch., 23, Langegasse. Y.M.C.A., 4, Belforter Vorstadt. At Illzach, near Mulhouse, Blind Asylum.

Munich.—C. and C.C.S., The Odeon, Rev. C. D. Blomfield. Wesl. Ch., Fürstenfelderstr. Y.M.C.A., 7, Landwehrstr.

Neuenahr.—S.P.G. (June 15 to August.)

NEU STRIESEN, near Dresden.—Mr. Otto Finger's work on 200 railway lines, among the employés of all grades.

NEUWIED-ON-THE-RHINE.—Moravian Settlement. Popular Bank (Central)—Raffeisen's System—Landwerthschaftliche Central Darlehnkasse.

Nuremberg.—C. and C.C.S. Baerischer Hof. Wesl. Ch. at 19, Spitalgasse, 9.30, and Weintraubenstr., 3 p.m.

Partenkirchen.—S.P.G. (July and August.)

POSEN.—London Jews' Soc., Rev. J. Lotka, 64, St. Martinstr.

Pyrmont.—C. and C.C.S. Meeting House, Rev. J. S. Owen.

Rummelsberg, near Berlin.—S.P.G. Rev. B. G. Durrad.

St. Goar.—C. and C.C.S. Lutheran Ch., Rev. H. T. Cavell.

Schwalbach.—C. and C.C.S. (From June to September.)

Schlangenbad.—S.P.G. (July 15 to September 15.)

SCHWABISCH-HALL.—Deaconesses' Institution.

Stettin.—Free Ch. Scotland (in summer). Bapt. Ch., 4, Johannisstr.
Y.M.C.A., 9, Elisabethstr.

Strasburg.—C. and C.C.S. Engl. Ch. French Free Ch., 16, Knoblochgasse, 11. French Ref. Ch., 11. Moravian Ch., 20, Niklaus Staden, 2. Episc. Meth. Ch., 4, Heleneng., 9.30 and 5.
Tract Dépôt, 12, Niklausstaden.

N.B.—The *Ban de la Roche* in the Vosges Mountains—the scene of Pastor Oberlin's work—may easily be reached from Strasburg ; rail to Rothau. Three miles further is Fouday (O.'s burial-place), and further on is Waldbach, where his study, etc., may be seen.

Stuttgart.—S.P.G., Olgastr., 10.30 and 4. Rev. L. R. Tuttiett.
Wesl. Meth. Ch., Sophienstr., Engl. Service at 10.30. Rev. W. Stevinson, 21, Olgastr.

STUTTGART :
Services in the Lutheran Chs. at 9.30 a.m., and at 2.30,
5, and 6 p.m. S. Schools at all the Chs.
The Royal Chapel, 10 and 5. Oberhofprediger, Herr
Prälat, K. von Gerok, Canzleistr., 21
Wesl. Ch., Sophienstr., 9.30, 3, and 8. S. Sch., 1.
Meth. Episc. Ch., Ulrichstr. and Schloss-str., 9.30 and 5.
Bapt. Ch., Hinterhaus, 16, Kasernenstr.
Brethren's Meeting (German), Blumenstr.
Evangelical Soc. Secretary, Rev. E. Falch, Faerberstr., 2.
Employs 7 City Missionaries and 9 travelling agents.
President of Y.M.C.A.'s in S. Germany is Rev. F. Reiff.
Christian Home for Travellers, 2, Gerberstr.
Brit. Jews' Soc.,'Rev. P. E. Gottheil, Militarstr., 87, III.
Stuttgart is celebrated for Educational Institutions.
The following may be mentioned :
Realgymnasium, 30, Lindenstr.
Karlsgymnasium, 14, Böblingerstr.
Realanstalt, 57, Langestr.
Katharinenstift (Girls), 34, Friederichstr.
Conservatorium for Music, 51, Langestr.
Triberg.—C. and C.C.S.
ULM.—Wesl. Meth. Ch., Roseng.
Wildbad.—S.P.G. (June to Sept.)
Weimar.—S.P.G., Bürgerschule, Rev. C. E. Harris.
Wiesbaden.—Engl. Episc. Ch. *Paülinenstift Retting-
haus.* Bible Stand in summer, near Kurhaus.
Bapt. Ch., 3, Schützenhofstr., 9.30 and 4.

Practical Christianity in Germany.

I. THE AGENCIES.

A. Numerous societies, and among them :
1. Evangelical Society for Germany (1848), President,
   Pastor Ohly, Elberfeld.
2. Rhenish Westphalian Provincial Com. for Inner
   Mission (1849). President, Professor Krüger,
   Langenberg.

B. Brothers' and Deacons' Establishments.
1. Rauhe Haus, Horn, near Hamburg (1833).
   Director, J. Wichern.
2. Züllchow, near Stettin (1850). President, G.
   Jahn.
3. Brecklum, near Bredstedt (Schleswig), 1879.
   Hausvater, G. Kaul. And others.

C. Deaconesses' Institutions.
1. Kaiserswerth-am-Rhein (1836). Director, Pastor
   Disselhof. 715 Sisters.
2. Strassburg (1842). Director, P. Fischer. 174
   Sisters.
3. Dresden (1844). President, Dr. Molwitz. 223
   Sisters.
4. Stuttgart (1854). Pastor Hoffmann. 307 Sisters
   and 40 others.

II. THE WORK.

A. Spiritual Destitution.
1. Work among Protestants living in Roman Catholic
   districts. Gustavus Adolph. S. (1832). President, Dr. Fricke, Leipzig.
2. Work among German Protestants in other lands.
   (*a*) Diaspora-Conferenz (1882). President, Dr.
   Trautvetter, Rudolstadt.
   (*b*) Lutheran Mission-Preacher Training School,
   Gross Ingarsheim, O. A. Besegheim, Würtemberg (1881). President, Professor Völter.
   (*c*) Promotion of Theological Studies. *Paulinum*
   in Berlin (1862). President, Rev. Schönfeld,
   Berlin. *Johanneum* in Berlin (1869). President, Prof. Kleinert, Berlin.
   (*d*) Bible Socs., 26.
   (*e*) Tract and Book Socs., 24.
   (*f*) Town Missions. Berlin (1877) (President,
   Hofprediger Stöcker), Bielefeld, Bremen,

Breslau, Dresden, Duisburg, Frankfurt-a.-M.,
Hamburg, Karlsruhe, Königsberg, Leipzig,
Liegnitz, and Magdeburg.

(*g*) Sunday School Socs. Com. for Germany (Secretary, Pred. Dr. Wachsman, Zionskirchstr., 31, Berlin, N.).

(*h*) Private Gymnasiums. Gütersloh (Westphalia), and Brecklum, near Bredstedt (Schleswig).

(*i*) Educational Institutes for Girls, mostly connected with Deaconesses' Institutions, 6 in number, one called Bon Pasteur being at Strassburg.

(*j*) School Socs. for Promoting Evangelical Teaching in Primary Schools, 13 in number.

(*k*) Christian Art Socs. Berlin (Graf v. Unruh, Burggrafenstr., 13, Berlin, W.), Würtemburg, Saxony, and Bavaria.

(*l*) Altar-cloth Socs. (*parament-vereine*), 8.

(*m*) Church-song Socs. for Germany (1882). Sec., Realgymn-Lehrer Th. Becker, Darmstadt.

B. Moral Dangers.

1. Saving the Lost.

   (*a*) Homes, more than 120 in all parts of the Empire.

   (*b*) Prisoners' Socs., 3.

   (*c*) Efforts against prostitution. 20 Magdalen Asylums, 3 temporary asylums, 4 Prevention Asylums, and 3 homes for mother and child ; 2 Anti-prostitution Socs., 4 asylums for confirmed girls in danger.

   (*d*) Efforts against drink. German Soc. against Abuse of Spirituous Drinks (1883), Secretary, Rev. Aug. Lammers, Bremen ; with many branches.

   (*e*) Central Total Abstinence Union (1884). President, Professor Dr. Rindfleisch, Trautenau, East Prussia ; with many branches.

(*f*) Asylums for drunkards, Lintorf, near Ratingen (Rhine provinces) ; for men, 27 beds. Director, Pastor Hirsch. And 3 others.

2. Guarding those in Peril.

(*a*) Socs. for education of the waifs and strays and others, 15.

(*b*) Working Men's Institutions. *Herberge zur Heimath*. The Herberge Socy. President, Dr. v. Bodelschwingh, Bethel, near Bielefeld. 12 branches. The *Herbergen* now number 327 in Germany.

(*c*) Young Men's Associations, 6.

(*d*) Associations of Young Merchants in Barmen, Bremen, Breslau, and Elberfeld, Frankfurt-a.-Main, Hamburg ('Excelsior'), Leipzig, Magdeburg, and M. Gladbach.

(*e*) Institutions for Girls (*Mägdeherbergen*), 36. Some are connected with schools and some with Hotels (Hospiz) for Ladies. One combining both is at Dresden, Holzhofgasse, 13, 14, and another at Frankfurt-a.-Main, *Marthaheim*, Bergstr., 58.

(*f*) Working Women's Institutions. Daheim für Arbeiterinnen, 7 Braustr., Leipzig, and 3 others.

(*g*) Sunday Socs. for Servant Girls, numerous.

(*h*) Working Colonies. At present 20 associations belong to the Central Association ; publishes a journal, *Arbeiter-Kolonie*. The Colonies are 16 in number. The first formed (1882) is at Wilhelmsdorf, near Bielefeld, Director, Pastor v. Bodelschwingh, Bielefeld.

(*i*) Asylums for Homeless, 8.

(*j*) Emigrants' Mission. President, Pastor Dr. Kreusler, Hamburg.

(*k*) Sailors' Mission, 4 socs.

C. Material Needs.
    (*a*) 1. For the sick, 22 homes.
        2. Hospitals for Children, 30 (one at Frank-
        furt-a.-M. and *Christ's Kinderhospital*).
        3. Healing Institute for Children. Mineral
        baths, 25 ; sea baths, 9 ; changes of
        climate, 3.
        4. Holiday Colonies—numerous committees.
        5. Blind Asylums.
        6. Idiot Asylums.
        7. Epileptic Asylums.   }Very numerous.
        8. Deaf and Dumb Asylums.
    (*b*) For the Poor—Crêches, Infant Schools.
    (*c*) Help in War-Times.

[The above is abbreviated from *Daheim-Kalender* for 888.]

(For further information see ' Leitfaden der Inneren Mission,' Von Th. Schäfer, Rauhe Haus, Hamburg. 250 pp., price 3 m. 60 pf.

Luther Tour.

Embracing the principal places connected with the life of the great Reformer.

    1.—Frankfort. At corner of Dom Platz, with Latin inscription *In silentio*, etc., is the house where Luther is said to have slept on his way to Worms.

    2.—Giessen. Our route brings us to this university town.

    3.—Marburg, the place of the memorable discussion between Luther and Zwingle.

    4.—Eisenach, where Luther went to school on leaving Mansfeld, and where he used to sing in the streets until Frau Ursula Cotta befriended him.

    5.—The Wartburg is near Eisenach, three or four miles distant. Here Luther sojourned under the pseudonym of Squire George.

    6.—Schmalkalden may be reached from Eisenach—railway to Wernhausen. There the famous League was formed.

7.—Erfurt, where Luther became an Augustinian monk. Here he first really studied the Bible and saw the truth of the Gospel.

8.—Weimar, associated with Goethe, and slightly so with Luther.

9.—Jena (University). In this town Luther's life was endangered through the opposition of the townsfolk.

10.—Eisleben, where he was born. The house still stands, and relics are shown. In St. Peter's Church he was baptized. In St. Andrew's is the pulpit in which he preached. Here, too, Luther died.

11.—Halle, where Luther lodged in the hostelry of the 'Golden Lock.' The University reminds one of Tholuck, a worthy successor of Luther in our time.

12.—Wittemberg, where Luther became a professor. Here, too, he finished translating the Bible. Outside the Elster Gate is an oak, planted on the spot where Luther burnt the Pope's bull in 1520. Here he was married. His dwelling in the Augustinian Convent is shown.

13. — Leipzig, where Auerbach's cellar is (Goethe's 'Faust'). Auerbach was Luther's great friend. At Leipzig the debate with Eck took place.

14.—Zwickau, where Luther preached from the balcony of Rathhaus to 25,000.

15.—Coburg, with its castle, where Luther is said to have written *Ein feste Burg*.

16.—Sonneberg is near Coburg—less than one hour by rail—with the house where Luther tarried more than once.

17.—Nürnberg, a queen of cities. Albert Dürer's home. Luther passed through it once.

18.—Augsburg. Diet held in 1530, and Augsburg Confession presented. This is still the Confession of the Lutheran Church.

19.—Ulm, with one of the finest Gothic cathedrals, but no reminiscence of Luther.

20.—Stuttgart, with many Christian institutions, but also not connected with Luther's history.

21.—Heidelberg. Luther twice came here—in 1510

and 1518. At Neuenheim, a village on the right bank of the Neckar, is the Mönchhof, where he is said to have lodged in 1518.

22.—Mannheim, for Worms, where the ever-famous Diet was held, to which Luther so boldly went.

23.—Oppenheim, near Worms, on the railway to Mayence. Here Luther received warning not to go to Worms. He is said to have slept at the Ritter Inn.

24.—Frankfort.

For full details of what may be seen at the various places included in this tour, see 'Homes and Haunts of Luther,' by the Rev. Dr. Stoughton (Religious Tract Society) ; also the various guide-books.

A circular ticket—Combinirbare Rundreisebillet—may be obtained at Frankfort, by writing out the list of places, and leaving it at the railway station or the Frankfurter Hof the day before the ticket is required. Cost, second class, about £4.

GERMAN UNIVERSITIES,

With names of some of the more prominent Theological Professors.

BERLIN.—Profs. B. Weiss, Dillmann, and Harnack.

BONN.—Prof. Christlieb.

ERLANGEN (Bavaria).—Stronghold of Lutheran orthodoxy: Profs. Frank, Kolde, and Sieffert.

GIESSEN.—Prof. Schürer.

GÖTTINGEN.—Profs. Schulz, Reuter, and Duhm (all of the Ritschl school).

GREIFSWALD.—Orthodox Lutheran : Profs. Zöckler, and Cremer.

HALLE.—Profs. Köstlin, Kähler, and Haupt.

HEIDELBERG. —*Advanced* Theology : Profs. Holsten, Hausrath, and Wendt.

LEIPZIG.— 693 Theological Students in 1887 : Profs. Delitzsch, Luthardt, and Zahn.

4

MARBURG.—Profs. Hermann and Kurz.
STRASSBURG.—Profs. Reuss and Holzmann.
TÜBINGEN.—Kübel and Weizsäcker.

SWITZERLAND.

Population (in 1888), 2,920,723. Protestants, 1,724,957 ; Roman Catholics (including Old Catholics), 1,190,008 ; Jews, 8,386.
Protestant Cantons are Vaud, Neuchâtel, Bâle, Schaffhausen, Zurich, and Glarus.
Roman Catholic Cantons : Freiburg, Valais, Tessin, Lucerne, Schwyz, Unterwalden, Uri, and Zug.
Appenzell is divided into Inner Rhodes (Roman Catholic) and Outer Rhodes (Protestant).
Mixed population : Geneva, Soleure, Aargau, Berne, Thurgau, St. Gall, and the Grisons.
The Jews are mostly found in Aargau.
The Reformed Ch. is divided into 3 sections. 1. The Zwinglian Section : Zurich, Thurgau, Glarus, St. Gall., Outer Rhodes, Grisons, and part of Schaffhausen. 2. The Calvinistic Section : Churches of French Switzerland (*Suisse Romande*) and partly of Berne. 3. The Œcolampadian Section—Bâle. All are supported by the State, except in Eastern Switzerland, where a tax is levied for the purpose.
Free Churches : 1. Free Evang. Ch. of Geneva. 2. Ind. Evang. Ch. of Geneva. 3. Free Ch. of Vaud. 4. Independent Evang. Ch. of Neuchâtel. 5. Various Independent Churches of Neuchâtel, 6. Baptist Chs., 1 chapel, 4 churches, 536 members, and 806 S. scholars. 7. Wesleyans in Vaud, etc. 8. Episc. Meth. Mission — 2 Districts : 1. Berne, District Elder, Leonhard Peter, Biel. 2. Zurich do., District Elder, H. Jacob Breiter, Kirchgasse, 50, Zurich. 28 ordained Swiss preachers, 4,846 members, 13,398 S. scholars. 9. Moravians in Zurich, Bâle, etc. 10. Various—Darbyites (Plym. Brethren) in Vaud and

Neuchâtel ; Anabaptists in the Juras and Neo-Baptists in Berne ; Evangl. Association (Albrecht's Brethren) in Berne ; Salvation Army, 2 Divisions, (1) Fr. Switzerland, Major Clibborn, 44*bis*, Rue Fendt Neuchâtel. 37 stations ; (2) German Switzerland, Major Patrick, Grünen Hof. Hottingen (Zurich), 19 stations.
AARGAU.—B. and F. Bible Soc. Dépôt. G. Angst. Aargau B. Soc.
BIASCA.—(Tessin) Chapel and Italian Evangelization. Pastor Calvino.
Baden (Swiss). —C. and C.C.S.
Bâle.—C. and C.C.S. at the Three Kings (June to Sept.). National Ch. Services at 9 a.m. at Cathedral, St. Peter's, St. Leonard's, and St. Theodore's (Petit-Bâle), at 11 for the young ; at 8 a.m. at St. Martin's, St. Alban's, and St. Elizabeth's, and the Orphan House (Waisenhaus).
French Ch., Temple, Holbein-Platz, 9 ; and at 5 in German.
Episc. Meth. Ch., 12, Wallstrasse, 9.30 and 5.
Four. Vereinshäuser. Services every Sunday. For hours of worship see local newspapers every Saturday.
University, Profs. C. J. Riggenbach, C. v. Orelli and Stockmayer.
Evangelical Union, 8, Spitalstrasse. Service, Sundays at 9 a.m.
Mission House—Principal, Inspector Oehler.
Bible and Tract Dépôt at Spittler's, Stapfelberg, 4.
St. Crischona Pilgrims' Mission, see List of German Missionary Socs.
Riehen Deaconesses' House. Director, Pastor Kügi.
Berne.—S.P.G., 12, Predigerstr., Rev. J. B. Smith.
National Ch. German, 9 a.m. ; French, 10.
Moravian Ch. (Brüder-Societät). German Service in choir of French Ch., 10.30.
Evangelical Soc. German Service in Vereinshaus, Nägeligasse, 9 and 7.30. Also Dépôt for Bibles and Tracts.

BERNE :
Free Ch., Ruelle des Prisons. French Service at
10.15 ; German at 8.45 a.m.
Episc. Meth. Ch., 61, Exterior Boulevard, Service at 9,
and 7.30.
University, Profs. Oettli, Müller, and Langhans.
Y.M.C.A., German, 212, Grande Rue. French, Baeren-
hofli.
B. and F. Bible Society's Depôt, Evang. Gesellschaft,
Nägeligasse.
CHUR, or COIRE.—Meth. Episc. Ch., 9.30 and 5.
Bibles at Depôt der Evang. Gesellschaft.
Geneva.—Engl. Episc. Ch., Holy Trinity, R. du Mont
Blanc, Rev. J. Last.
Est. Ch. of Scotland. In the 2 summer months in the
Cath. St. Pierre.
Amer. Episc. Emanuel Ch., Rue des Voirons, 10.30 a.m.
Eglise Nationale de Genève. Cath. St. Pierre, St. Ger-
vais ; Fusterie, Madeleine, Eaux-Vives, Plainpalais,
Pâquis, all at 10.
Culte organisé par l'Union Nat. Evang. Petite Salle de
la Réformation, 65, Rue du Rhône, 10. German
Services all at 10.
Meth. Ep. Ch., 9, Rue des Granges, Pastor Brändle.
Italian Meth. Ep. Ch., 10 a.m., Fusterie 7, Rev. T. Malan.
Italian Evangelization, 26, Rive, Friday, 8 p.m.
Evangelical Free Ch., Oratoire, Rue Tabazan, 9 and 8 ;
and Rue Levrier, 10 and 7.
Independ. Ch., 20, Rue de la Pelisserie, 10 and 8.
Evangelical Congregation, 7, Rue des Buis Pâquis, 10 ;
Temperance Mg., Wednesday Evg.
Salles d'Evangelisation, 26, Rue de Rive, Sunday at
2.30, Friday at 8, and 4 other Salles.
Rel. Tract Society's Dépôt, Rue Verdaine, 9.
Y.M.C.A.—French, 2, Place du Port ; German, 23,
Gde. Rue.
Soc. for Sanctification of Sunday. Secretary, Pastor
Deluz, 9, Rue Candolle.

Geneva :

Swiss Temperance Soc. Office, 7, Rue de l'Evêché.

University. Bastions. Professors of Theology, Oltra-mare, Bouvier, and others.

Theological Faculty of Evangelical Soc., Oratoire, Rue Tabazan, Professors Tissot, Ruffet, and Barde.

Evangelical Soc., Oratoire. Secretary, Pastor Rimond, Rue Tabazan. Stations and colporteurs in France.

National Evangelical Union. Secretary, M. A. Bour-dillon, 2, Bould. du Théâtre.

Popular Evangelization. Secretary, M. E. Favre, 6, Rue des Granges.

Salvation Army, 5, Rue de Rive.

B. and F. Bible Dépôt, Robert Frères, Pl. Bel Air.

Heinrichsbad near Herisau.—A place of rest for Christians. Director, Pastor Wenger.

Lausanne.—Engl. Episc. Ch. Christ Church, 10.30 and 4.

Presb. Ch., Trinity Ch., Avenue de Rumine, 10.30 and 4, Rev. A. F. Buscarlet. Bible-class, Wedny. 4 p.m. (90 or 100 attendance) ; and for young men, Sunday 8 p.m.

National Ch., Secy. of Synod, Pasteur Würsten, La Tour de Peilz.

Free Ch., Chap. des Terreaux, at 9 ; Chap. de Mar-theray, 10.30. President of Synodal Commission, Pastor S. Burnier, Lutry.

Wesl. Ch. (French), 1, Rue du Valentin, Pl. de la Riponne, 9.30 and 7.30.

Independent Ch., Pastor Byse, service at Athénée 4 p.m.

Bible Dépôt, 1, Rue Madeleine.

Rel. Tract Society's Dépôt, Imprimerie G. Bridel, Pl. de la Louve.

Theological Faculty of National Church, Professors L. Durand, Dandirand, and Combe.

Theological Faculty of Free Ch., Professors Astié Bovon, and Ch. Porret.

S. East African Mission of Free Ch., Secretary M. P. Leresche, Lausanne.

Lucerne.—C. and C.C.S., April to Oct., in Swiss Prof. Ch.

Presb. Ch., 11 and 6, in Maria Hilf Ch.

French Service in Salle Presbytérale of Ref. Ch.

Bible and Tract Depôt. A. Uhlmann, 43, Zürichesstr.

MÄNNEDORF.—Canton of Zurich. Establishment for cure of disease by Prayer. Director, Herr Zeller.

Montreux.—Engl. Episc. Ch.

Presb. Ch., Oct. to June, 11 and 4, Rev. P. Fisher in winter.

National Ch., 10 and 2. Free Ch., 9 and 5.

MONTMIRAIL, by Neuchâtel.—Moravian Church, Pastor Reichel. Also at Peseux, Chaux-de-fonds and Le Locle.

NEUCHÂTEL.—C. and C.C.S., Rue de la Collégiale, 11 and 4.30.

National Ch., Collégiale, 9.45. German Service, Temple du Bas, 9 a.m. President of Synod, Pastor Dubois, Neuchâtel.

Nat. Theological Faculty, in the Academy, Profs. Du Bois, Perrochet, and Morel.

Eng. Indépendante, Temple du Bas—Rue du Temple Neuf, 10.30 ; Chap. de l'Ermitage, 9.30 and 8 ; and Salle des Conférences, 8.o.

Free Church (French), Place d'Armes, 10 and 8.

Theological Faculty of Independent Ch. Professors Dr. Godet, G. Godet, and Gretillat.

Meth. Episc. Ch., 6, Rue de l'Hôpital, 9.30 and 8.

German Evangelization. Meeting, Sunday evening, 8.

Salvation Army, 5, Rue de l'Ecluse.

B. and F. Bible Soc. Librairie. Delachaux and Niestlé.

Temperance Society, Ancienne Tonhalle, Friday, 8.

Temperance Inns. Auberge et Pension, R. de Pommier ; Pension Ouvrière, R des Moulins, and Café et Pension de la Croix-Bleue, R. des Fausses-Brayes et des Terreaux.

ST. GALLEN.—Episc. Meth. Ch., 9.30 and 5. French Ch., Katharinen Kapelle, 9.

B. and F. Bible Dépôt, C. Stolz, Ev. Gesellschaft.

Vevey.—C. and C.C.S., Engl. Ch. Rev. G. Akehurst.
National Ch., St. Martin (from May to Oct.), 9.30 a.m.,
Ste. Claire (Oct. to May), 10 a.m. ; and all the year
round at 7.30 p.m.
Free Ch., Rue du Panorama, 9.30 a.m. summer, 10
a.m. winter, and 7.30 p.m.
Wesl. Ch. (French).

Zurich.—Engl. Episc. Ch., 10.30 and 4.30.
National Ch. (German), 8.30 in summer.
French Service, 13, Kirchgasse, 9 a.m.
German Evangelical Ch. St. Anna, 8.30 in summer,
and 5.
Meth. Episc. Ch., Promenadestr., 9 and 5.
University. Profs. Häring, Fritzsche, and Volkmar.
Y.M.C.A., 2, Augustinerhof.
B. and F. Bible Soc., Ev. Gesellschaft, 13, Kirchgasse.
Christian Hotel, ' Widder,' 1, Rennweg.
At Neumünden, near Zürich, Inst. for Epileptics,
Director, Herr Koelle.

ENGLISH SERVICES IN SUMMER.

SWITZERLAND.

Aigle (C. and C.C.S.)
Andermatt (S.P.G.)
Axenstein (S.P.G.)
Arolla (C. and C.C.S.)
Beatenberg (C. and C.C.S.)
Ballaigues (C. and C.C.S.)
Bel Alp (S.P.G.)
Berival (S.P.G.), Aug.
Bex (C. and C.C.S.)
Brunnen (C. and C.C.S.)
Campfer (S.P.G.)
Chamouni (C. and C.C.S.)
Champery Valais (C. and
C.C.S.)
Château d'Oex (C. and
C.C.S.)

Chaumont (C. and C.C.S.)
Chexbres (C. and C.C.S.)
Clarens (C. and C.C.S.)
Coire (C. and C.C.S.)
Comballaz aux Ormonts
(C. and C.C.S.)
Davos-am-Platz (C. and
C.C.S.)
Diablerets (C. and C.C.S.)
Disentis (C. and C.C.S.)
Divonne-les-Bains (C. and
C.C.S.)
Eggischorn (C. and C.C.S.)
Engelberg (S.P.G.)
Evolène (C. and C.C.S.)
Felsenegg (C. and C.C.S.)

Generoso (C. and C.C.S.)
Gersau, Canton Schwyz, (S.P.G.), May to Oct.
Giessbach (C. and C.C.S.)
Glion (C. and C.C.S.), May to Oct.
Grindelwald(C. and C.C.S.)
Heiden (C. and C.C.S.)
Hospenthal (S.P.G.)
Interlaken (C. and C.C.S.), May to Oct. Presb. Ch., June to Sept., 11 and 4; also French Service
Kandersteg (S.P.G.)
Le Prese (C. and C.C.S.)
Les Avants (C. and C.C.S.), April to Sept.
Leuk (C. and C.C.S.)
Locarno (C. and C.C.S.)
Lugano (S.P.G.), April to Oct.
Macolin (C. and C.C.S.)
Macugnaga (S.P.G.), Aug. to Sept.
Maderanerthal (C. and C.C.S.)
Maloja (S.P.G.)
Mürren (S.P.G.)
Pontresina (S.P.G.), Holy Trinity Presb. Ch., in village Ch., 11.
Promontogno (C. and C.C.S.)
Ragatz (C. and C.C.S.). Also French Service in Chap. Evangélique
Rheinfelden (S.P.G.)
Rhone Glacier (C. and C.C.S.)
Rieder Alp (S.P.G.)
Riffel Alp (C. and C.C.S.)
Righi-Dailly (S.P.G.), Aug.

Rigi-Kaltbad (C. and C.C.S.)
Rigi-Scheideck (S.P.G.)
Rosenlaui (S.P.G.)
Rossinières (C. and C.C.S.)
Saas Fèe (C. and C.C.S.)
Saas Grunde (S.P.G.)
Samaden (C. and C.C.S.)
Seelisburg (S.P.G.)
Sonnenberg (S.P.G.), Aug.
Spiez (C. and C.C.S.)
St. Gervais (C. and C.C.S.)
St. Luc (C. and C.C.S.)
Stachelberg (C. and C.C.S.)
St. Moritz (S.P.G.), June to April. Presb. Ch., July to Sept. 7; in Eglise Evangélique, 3.30; also French Service
Silva Plana (S.P.G.), July to Aug. 31
Tarasp (C. and C.C.S.)
Thun (C. and C.C.S.); also French Service in Chap. de Scherzlingen
Thusis (C. and C.C.S.)
Uetliberg (C. and C.C.S.)
Vernayaz (S.P.G.), Aug.
Villars-sur-Ollon (C. and C.C.S.)
Villeneuve (C. and C.C.S.)
Weissenstein (S.P.G.)
Weisshorn, Valais (S.P.G.)
Wengern Alp (C. and C.C.S.)
Wesen Wallensee (C. and C.C.S.)
Wiesen (S.P.G.), March to May
Zermatt (C. and C.C.S.)
Zinal (C. and C.C.S.)
Zutz (C. and C.C.S.)

ITALY.

Population (1887) 30,260,065. Protestants in 1881 estimated at 62,000 (of whom 22,000 in the Valleys); Jews 38,000.

Protestant Churches:

1. Waldensian, (*a*) in the Valleys, 24 pastors and 13,289 members. (*b*) Evangelistic Mission in the rest of Italy, 44 churches, 44 stations, and 4,074 members. President, Rev. M. Prochet, 107, Via Nazionale, Rome.
2. Free Italian Church, 15 ordained ministers, 12 evangelists, and 1,522 members. Treasurer, Rev. J. R. McDougall, Chiesa Scozzese, Florence.
3. Wesleyan Methodists, 25 Italian ministers, 10 chapels, and 35 other preaching places : 1,344 members. President of Northern District, Rev. H. J. Piggott, 21, Via delle Coppelle, Rome ; President of Southern District, Rev. T. W. S. Jones, Largo, S. Anna, Naples.
4. Episcopal Methodists, 24 ministers and 920 members. President of Northern District, Mr. W. Burt, 24, V. Lorenzo il Magnifico, Florence. President of Southern District, Sig. G. B. Gattuso, 2, Piazza Poli, Rome.
5. Baptist Apostolical Christian Union, 22 principal stations, 30 ministers and evangelists, and 875 members. President, Rev. Jas. Wall, 35, Piazza di S. Lorenzo in Lucina, Rome.
6. Free, or Brethren Church, 28 principal stations.

ALESSANDRIA.—Italian Services, Meth. Ep. Ch., Via Verona. Brethren Service, 9, Via Vittoria.

Amalfi.—S.P.G. February to April.

ANCONA.—Wald. Ch., 53, Via Calamo.

Andorno, near Biella.—S.P.G. April 15 to Sept.

ANGROGNA.—Wald. Ch., Tempio Valdese.

AOSTA.—Wald. Ch., 7, R. Croix de Ville.

ASOLO (province of Treviso).—Popular Bank (1873), the first of many now at work in the province.

BASSIGNANA.—Free Ch., 1, Via Ospedale.

Bellagio.—C. and C.C.S. St. James', April to Oct.

BERGAMO.—Free Ch., 9, Via S. Bernardino. Germ. Ref. Ch., Piazza della Fiera.

Bordighera.—Engl. Ep. Ch., Wald. Ch., Villa Lozeron. At Vallecrosia, Mrs. Boyce's Evangelical Institute for Boys and Girls.

Bologna.—S.P.G. Hôtel Brun, March 1 to May 31, and Oct. to Nov., Rev. M. R. Neligan.

Italian Services : (1) Free Ch., 23, Via Ugo Bassi, 12 and 7.30.

  (2) Wesl. Ch., 5, Via S. Vitale.

  (3) Meth. Episc. Ch., Tempio Evangelico, behind Palazzo Comunale.

  (4) Baptist Ch., Piazza Malpighi.

  (5) Brethren's Mg., 116, Ripa di Reno.

Bormio.—S.P.G. July to Sept. 15.

BRESCIA.—Wald. Ch., 2770, Via Cappuccini, at 11.

BRINDISI.—Wald. Ch., Salita S. Dionisio.

Cadenabbia.—S.P.G. March to Oct. 31.

Capri.—S.P.G. Jan. to March.

Castellamare.—C. and C.C.S., in winter. Wesl. Ch.

CATANIA.—Wald. Ch., 14, Strada Naumachia. Wesl. Ch., Strada Lincoln.

CIVITAVECCHIA.—Bapt. Ch., 3, Via Adriani.

COMO.—Wald. Ch., Via Allessandro Volta.

Cornigliano.—C. and C.C.S. In winter.

Courmayeur.—C. and C.C.S. Wald. Ch., R. du Mont Blanc.

CREMONA.—Wesl. Ch., Via Milazzo.

CRESPANO.—Hospital for persons suffering from *Pellagra* (species of leprosy, result of eating only maize).

DOMODOSSOLA.—Wesl. Ch., 170, Via Sempione.

Florence.—Engl. Episc. Ch., Via La Marmora, Rev. R. L. Tottenham ; and 18, Via Maggio, Rev. C. Tooth, 11 and 3.

  Presb. Ch., 11, Lung' Arno Guicciardini, 11 and 4, Rev. J. R. McDougall, Treasurer of Free Ital. Ch. Sept. 15 to July.

FLORENCE:
Amer. Episc. Ch., 11, Piazza del Carmine, Rev. E. B.
Russel.
French and German Ch., 9, Lung' Arno Guicciardini.
Italian Services : (1) Wald. Ch., 51, Via dei Serragli,
11 a.m. ; and 11, Via Manzoni.
(2) Free Ch., 7, Via dei Benci, 11 and 8.
(3) Meth. Episc. Ch., 2, Via S. Gallo.
(4) Bapt. Ch., 6, Piazza S. Trinita.
(5) Brethren's Meeting, 17, Via della Vigna Vecchia.
Waldensian Theological College, 51, Via dei Serragli,
Profs. Dr. Geymonat and Dr. Comba, 13 students.
Meth. Episc. Theol. Ch., 24, V. Lor. il Magnifico.
Director, Rev. E. S. Stackpole.
Evangelical Schools : (1) Waldensian, 33, Via Maffia.
(2) Free Ch., 7, Via dei Benci.
Protestant Industrial Home for Boys, 6, Via Aretina.
Director, Dr. Comandi ; also Evangelistic Hall.
Deaconesses' Teaching Institute, 41, Via Sta. Monaca.
S. Frediano Mission, Borgo Stella, 9.
Medical Mission, 6, Via Piazza Cavour, Miss Roberts,
Director.
Evangelical Hospital, Villa Betania, Poggio Imperiale.
Tract Dépôt, and Claudian Press of Ev. Publication
Soc., Via dé Serragli. Secretary, Rev. J. B. Will, 33,
Via Maffia.
B. and F. Bible Soc. Dépôt, 15, Via dei Panzani.
The Agent of the B. and F. Bible Soc. for Italy and
Malta, Rev. A. Meille, resides at Florence, 124, Via
dei Serragli, third floor.
Superior Institute—Faculties of Philosophy and Science
and Languages.
Genoa.—Engl. Episc. Ch., Via Goito, Rev. A. E. Carey.
Presb. Ch., 4, Via Peschiera, at 11. Rev. Donald Miller.
German Protestant Ch., near Waldensian Ch.
French Reformed Ch., Via Curtatone.
Italian Services : (1) Wald. Ch., Via Assarotti, 10.30.
Also Schools.

GENOA :

(2) Free Ch., 46, Via Giulia, 11 and 8.

(3) Bapt. Ch., 36, Piazza Deferrari.

(4) Wesl. Ch., Galleria Mazzini.

(5) Brethren's Meeting, 5, Via della Vigne.

Floating Bethel, Steam Launch in Harbour, the *Caledonia.* (Genoa Harbour Mission, Rev. Donald Miller, Secretary, 4, Via Peschiera ; Missionary, Capt. P. Clucas.)

Seamen's Institute, 26, Via Milano. Rev. A. E. Carey.

B. and F. Bible Soc. Dépôt, 9, Via Assarotti.

Swiss School, 10, S. Bartolomeo degli Armeni.

German School, 30, Via Assarrotti.

Lanzo d'Intelvi.—S.P.G. (August to September.)

Leghorn (Livorno).—Engl. Episc. Ch., at 11, 17, Via degli Elisi. Rev. H. H. Irvine.

Presb. Ch., 3, Via degli Elisi, 11. Rev. J. Macfarlane. And at Bethel at 7 p.m.

Italian Services : (1) Wald. Ch., Piazza Manin, 11 and 8.

(2) Free Ch., 8, Via Asili, 11 and 7.

(3) Bapt. Ch., 2, Via dei Fulgidi.

German Ch., 3, Scali Olandesi.

Sailors' Institute. Supt., Rev. J. Macfarlane, 10, Vico Cotels.

Sailors' Reading Room, La Fortezza del Molo Vecchio.

B. and F. Bible Soc. Dépôt, 8, Via S. Francesco.

LIDO.—Sanatorium for Sickly Scrofulous Children—21 such establishments in Italy, 13 on the Mediterranean, and 8 on the Adriatic.

Lucca.—Wald. Ch., 18, Via Galli Tassi.

Baths of Lucca, Engl. Episc. Ch.

Malta.—Ch. of England, St. Paul's and Holy Trinity, Sliema. Services at Garrison Chapels, Dockyard Chapel, and Hospital Chapels.

Presb. Ch., Stra Mezzodi, 11 and 6 ; and Military Chapel, S. Margherita, 8.45 and 6.

B. and F. Bible Soc. Dépôt, 26, Piazza Miratore, Floriana.

MALTA :
B. and F. Sailors' Soc. Steam Launch. Supt., Capt.
R. Stephens, 19, Piazza Miratore, Floriana.
MANTUA.—Wald. Ch. Pal. Guerrieri—Gonzaga, Via
Marmorini.
Brethren's Meeting, 17, Via Tubo.
Maiori.—S.P.G. (January 15 to April.)
Menazzio.—S.P.G. (May, June, and September.)
MARSALA.—Wesl. Ch., Via Rubino.
Messina (Sicily).—C. and C.C.S. Rev. J. J. Varnier.
Italian Churches : (1) Wald. Ch., Via Monte di Pietà.
(2) Wesl. Ch. Pal. Falletti.
Rev. J. J. Varnier, 35, Via S. Marta, and Signor
Scuderi, carry on Evangelical work.
Missionary to Sailors, Rev. J. J. Varnier.
Milan.—C. and C.C.S., 8, Via Andegari. Rev. T. A. Lindon.
Lutheran Ch., Via Carlo Porta.
Italian Services : (1) Wald. Ch., S. Giovanni in Conca,
Via Carlo Alberto, 11 and 8.
(2) Free Ch., 13, Via San Simone, 12.30 and 8.
(3) Wesl. Ch., 38, Via Broletto.
(4) Bapt. Ch., 39, Via del Pesce.
(5) Meth. Episc. Ch., 7, Via Val Petrosa.
(6) Brethren's Meeting, 10, Via Unione.
Bible Dépôt, 31, Via Carlo Alberto.
MODENA.—Meth. Episc. Ch., Via della Torre.
Bapt. Ch., 18, Via Emilia.
Nervi.—C. and C.C.S. in winter.
Naples.—Engl. Episc. Ch., Strada S. Pasquale, 11 and
3.15. Rev. H. T. Barff.
Presb. Ch., 2, Cappella Vecchia, 11 and 3.30. Rev. T.
J. Irving.
Wesl. Ch., Largo S. Anna di Palazzo. Rev. T. W. S. Jones.
French and German Services, Egl. Française, Vico
Carlo Poerio.
Italian Services : (1) Wald. Ch., S. Tommaso, 11.30
and 8 ; and Evangelistic work at 31, Piazza Prin-
cipe Umberto.

NAPLES :

  (2) Free Ch., 7, Vico Medina, Guantai Nuovi, 12 and 8.
  (3) Wesl. Ch., Largo S. Anna di Palazzo, 11.30 and 7.
  (4) Bapt. Chs., 175, Via Foria, and Piazza S.
      Domenico Maggiore.
  (5) Meth. Episc. Ch., 17, Via Nilo.
  Italian Protestant Day Schools at the various Protes-
      tant Chapels.
  Harbour Mission, B. and F. Sailors' Society, Floating
      Bethel. Supts., Rev. J. Irving, 2, Cappello Vecchia,
      and Mr. D. J. Cartney, 118, Rione Amadeo.
  Bible and Tract Dépôt, 101, Via di Chiaia.
  University. Lectures free. Political Economy. 1
      professor and 8 assistant professors. (*Privati
      insegnanti.*) Altogether, 206 professors.
  German School, 60, Egiziana a Pizzofalcone.
  MacKean Bentinck Institute, Via Amadeo ; 165 pupils.
  International School, 26, S. Carlo a Mortelli ; 118 pupils.

Nervi.—C. and C.C.S. in winter.

Ospedaletti.—C. and C.C.S. in winter.

PADUA.—Wesl. Ch., 4121, Via Rovina.

Palermo.—Engl. Episc. Ch., Via Stabile. Rev. Dr. T.
    Dixon.
  Italian Services : (1) Wald. Ch., 36, Via Macqueda,
      Palazzo Cutò.
  (2) Free Ch., Pal. Campofranco, 8, Croce dei Vespri.
  (3) Wesl. Ch., 2, Via S. Chiara.
  (4) Meth. Episc. Ch., 79, Piazza Marina.
  B. and F. Bible Soc. Dépôt, 16, Via Macqueda.

Pallanza—C. and C.C.S., Grand Hotel.

PARMA.—Wesl. Ch., 13, Borgo Cappello.

PAVIA.—Wesl. Ch., Via Morazzone.

Pegli.—S.P.G. Rev. A. C. Jackson.

PERUGIA.—Ep. Meth. Ch., 13, Via Priori.

PIACENZA.—Wesl. Ch., 13, Via S. Pietro.

PIGNEROL.—Wald. Ch.
  B. and F. Bible Soc. Dépôt. Signor C. B. Ribetti,
    Tempio Valdese.

Pisa.—Engl. Episc. Ch., from October to May. Rev. R. Johnson.

Italian Services : (1) Wald. Ch., 9, Via del Museo, 11.

(2) Free Ch., Piazzetti dei Grilletti, 11 and 8.

(3) Meth. Ep. Ch., Tempio Evangelico, Via S. Sepolcro.

Italian Day Schools at Pisa and Cisanello, under direction of Miss Carruthers, 5, Via del Santo, Cisanello.

Pozzuoli.—C. and C.C.S. Wesl. Ch., Casa Manduca.

Rapallo and **Sta. Margherita.**—S.P.G. Dec. 15 to April.

RAVENNA.—Ital. Brethren Mg., 15, Via Baccinetti.

Rome.—Engl. Episc. Ch. (1) S.P.G., All Saints', Via del Babuino, Rev. H. N. Wasse. (2) Trinity Ch., Piazza San Silvestro, Rev. E. Cowan.

Amer. Episc. Ch., St. Paul's, Via Nazionale, Rev. Dr. Nevin.

Presb. Ch., 7, Via Venti Settembre, 11 and 3, Rev. Dr. G. Gray. October 15 to June 15.

Lutheran Ch., Pal. Caffarelli, Rev. C. K. Roenneke.

Italian Services : (1) Wald. Ch., 107, Via Nazionale, 11 and 7.30.

(2) Free Ch., Piazza Ponte S. Angelo, 11 and 7.30 ; and Day School.

(3) Wesl. Ch., 63, Via della Scrofa. Military Ch., 28, Via delle Coppelle.

(4) Bapt. Ch., 35, Piazza San Lorenzo in Lucina ; 26, Via del Teatro Valle ; 154, Via Urbana ; and 6 other meeting-places.

(5) Meth. Episc. Ch., 2, Piazza Poli.

Evangelical Mission, 6, Via Marco Minghetti, Major Colquhoun.

Gould Memorial Industrial Home, 18, Via Magenta.

Anglo-Roman Institute, 145, Via Rasella, 51 pupils.

German School, Campidoglio, Palazzo Caffarelli.

Evangelical Hospital, 26, Via di Monte Tarpeo.

London Jews' Soc., Mrs. Burtchaell, 50, Via S. Niccolò da Tolentino ; Mr. P. E. Arias, Via Conteverde, 15.

B. and F. Bible Soc. Dépôt, 51, Via Capo le Case.

Tract Dépôt, 62, Via della Scrofa.

S. Remo.—C. and C.C.S. St. John Bapt. in winter, and All Saints'. Un. Presb. Ch., Rev. J. Robertson, winter, Casa Vareglia ; Germ. Luth. Ch., Corso Garibaldi ; Wald. Ch., Corso Umberto, 9.

SALERNO.—Wesl. Ch., 106, Corso Garibaldi.

San Dalmazzo di Tenda, near Nice, S.P.G., May and June.

Sestri Ponente.—C. and C.C.S., Gd. Hotel.

Sienna.—S.P.G., March to May, Ital. Independ. Ch.

Sorrento.—S.P.G., Nov. to May.

Spezia.—S.P.G., Nov. to Feb.
Italian Services : (1) Bapt. Ch., Casa Alberto, Piazza Vitt. Emanuele, at 11. Also 20 stations, superintended by Rev. E. Clarke, 150 members.
(2) Wesl. Church, Via da Passano.
(3) Free Ch., 5, Via Calatafimi, 11 and 4.

Stresa.—C. and C.C.S., April to Oct., Hot. des Iles Borromées.

SYRACUSE.—Wesl. Ch., Via Gargallo.

Taormina (Sicily).—Ch. of Engl. occasional.

TORRE PELLICE, or La Tour, in Waldensian Valleys, Waldensian Ch. Bapt. Ch., Via Angrogna.
Independ. Ch., Via del Centro.
Waldensian College (1835), general education, 50 pupils and 7 teachers.
B. and F. Bible Soc. Dépôt, Signor B. Goss, Via di Francia.

Turin.—C. and C.C.S., 15, Via Pio Quinto.
Italian Services : (1) Wald. Ch., Tempio Valdese, Corso del Re, 11 (French) and 3 (Italian).
(2) Bapt. Ch., 44, Via Cernaia.
(3) Meth. Episc. Ch., 27, Via Maria Vittoria.
(4) Brethren's Mg., 20, Via Cavour.
College for Waldensian Artisans, 34, Via Bartholdi, 38 pupils.
B. and F. Bible Soc. Dépôt, 15, Via Pio Quinto.

Varese.—C. and C.C.S., April to Oct. Rev. E. Cowan, Grand Hotel.

VENICE.—S.P.G., Grand Hotel, Rev. J. Scarth, Un. Presb. Ch., 95, Piazza S. Marco, April to July.

VENICE :

Lutheran Ch., Scuola dell' Angelo Custode.

Italian Services : (1) Wald. Ch., Palazzo Cavagnis, 12.
(2) Free Ch., 95, Piazza San Marco, 12.30 and 8 ;
and Chiesa Sta. Margherita, 12.30 and 8.
(3) Meth. Episc. Ch., 4,233, Piazza Manin.
(4) Bapt. Ch., 2,132 Campo Mater Domini.

Ragged Industrial School, 993, Canareggio, S. Giobbe,
founded by Mrs. Hammond.

Sailors' Mission, M. J. J. Whitehead, 399, Calle del
Rimedio, Vicino Chiesa S. Marco.

QUERINI.—Stampalia Institute, Free Library.

Verona.—C. and C.C.S., Sept. to Oct. Wald. Ch., Via
Duomo, al Canto di Via Pigna.

Viareggio.—Engl. Ep. Ch., Wesl. Ch., 2, Via del Giardino.

Villa d'Este.—C. and C.C.S., April to Oct. Rev. H. L.
Dixon.

ON THE TRACK OF THE REFORMERS.

The Reformation did not take hold of Italy. It had its
adherents in many places, but it never became a general
movement. There were, however, men and women of
note who identified themselves with it. Italy, too, is
the home of the Waldenses, and the scene of their heroic
struggles and bitter sorrows. Nor should we forget men
like Savonarola, Giordano Bruno, and others who, though
not Protestants, yet rose up to protest against the errors
and corruptions of Rome. The traveller, therefore, who
is interested in the great religious conflict of the fifteenth
and sixteenth centuries will find himself, as he traverses
the Peninsula, coming again and again to places redolent
of hallowed memories. In the Valleys of Piedmont
everything around him will call to mind the Waldenses.

Train from Turin to Pignerol, and thence by omnibus
to La Tour—the chief town. The Pra del Tor echoed
in 1560 with the shout, ' *Viva Jesu Cristo*,' as the Waldenses stood up to defend their homes. In 1561 a great

5

gathering in the Valley of Perouse pledged themselves to try and maintain their liberties and rights. The rugged ravine of the Rorá is another memorable spot where the heroic people contrived methods of defence. Aosta was the birthplace of St. Anselm, and of the St. Bernard who founded the hospice that bears his name. A stone here records the flight of Calvin in 1541.

In Ferrara, Calvin and Clément Marot, the psalm-writer, sojourned at the Court of the Duchess Renée. The celebrated Olympia Morata, the most learned lady of her day and a devout Christian, lived here.

At Lucca, the marble pulpit in the Cathedral recalls the memory of Peter Martyr Vermiglio, whose Evangelical sermons were listened to by crowded congregations. In Lucca, too, Aonio Paleario, the most prominent of the Italian Reformers, was classical professor for a time.

Of Savonarola and Florence we need hardly speak. There are the convent of S. Marco, where his cell and various relics are shown ; the Duomo, where his wonderful sermons were often preached ; the Piazza, where he erected 'the Pyramid of Vanities,' and where afterwards he was himself consumed by fire ; the Bargello, now a museum, where he was imprisoned ; and the Villa Carreggi, where he had the well-known interview with Lorenzo de Medici.

In Sienna we come upon traces of Bernardino Ochino, 'whose sermons,' said Charles V., 'can move stones to tears ;' and of Vittoria Colonna, another of the honourable and learned women of the day, whose hearts were drawn out towards the Gospel.

The city of Rome saw but little of the Reform movement, but Luther went there a believer in the Pope, and left it an unbeliever.

Naples reminds one of the Spaniard Juan Valdés, whose expositions of Scripture and other writings did great service, and who gathered around him for the study of Scripture, in his house on the Bay, such men as Ochino and Carnesecchi. Ladies, too, were present, and especially Giulia Gonzaga Colonna, for whose benefit he wrote his *Alfabeto Cristiano.*

In the wild region of Calabria, at San Sisto, on the road to Cosenza, and elsewhere, were several colonies of Waldensians, who for a while found a quiet home there, until at last the relentless foe of the truth drowned them in blood. Traditions of the old times linger there, as also many traces of the Angrognese dialect which they spoke.

Venice had its confessors. For a time a Church of believers existed there, and was visited by reformers from Geneva and elsewhere. But the Inquisition was at last permitted to do its work, and so one after another of the faithful were dropped into the deep water over against the Arsenal. [See Dr. Stoughton's 'Footprints of the Italian Reformers.' Rel. Tract Soc.]

SPAIN.

Population (1886), 16,733,200.

Bibles, etc., in Spanish, are obtainable at each place mentioned below.

Barcelona.—C. and C.C.S. Engl. Ch., Rev. H. L. Downman.

Spanish Services :

(1) Lausanne Committee, 15, Conde de Asalto. Pastor Empaytaz, 341, Calle de las Cortes.

(2) Wesl. Meth., 10, Abaixadores. Rev. Mr. Simpson, Director. Methodist Missions in Spain and Gibraltar : 8 preaching places, 4 ministers, and 278 members. In Balearic Isles : 11 chapels, 3 ministers, and 116 members.

(3) Brethren's Mission, Calle san Gabriel, Gracia.

(4) Amer. Bapt. Mission, Past. Lund. Services also at Hospitalet.

Bookshop, 15, Conde de Asalto. Bible Soc. Dépôt, 19, Calle Buenavista, Gracia.

Bilbao.—C. and C.C.S. Rev. A. Burnell. Occasional Services. Every Sunday at Portugalete.
Sp. Prot. Services, Pastor Marqués.
B. and F. Sailors' Soc., Seamen's Hall, San Nicolas. Missionary, Mr. G. Phillipson (private address, Apertado, 192). Sailors' Institute also at Luchana.

Cadiz.—Engl. Episc. Ch.
Spanish Evangelization Soc., 6, Calle Teneria.

CARTAGENA.—Dutch Mission. Pastor D. F. Orejon, 16, Calle de San Diégo.

CORDOVA.—Irish Presb. Ch., 12, Candelaria.

CORUNNA.—Brethren's Mission.

FIGUERAS.—Pastor Lopez-Rodriguez' Mission Ch. and and 7 other stations.

Gibraltar.—Engl. Episc. Ch.
Presb. Ch., St. Andrew's, 11 and 6. Wesl. Ch., morning and evening. Bible and Tract Dépôt, Mr. Fromow, Church Street.

Granada.—S.P.G. in spring. Spanish Service, 7, Calle Tendillas, Past. Alhama.

Huelva.—Sp. Evang. Soc., 30, Mendez Nuñez. Engl. Service at 11.

JEREZ DELA FRONTERA.—Un. Presb. Mission, Ch. and Schools, Vallesequillo.

Madrid.—Engl. Episc. Ch.
German Service : German Legation. Pastor Fliedner.
Spanish Services :
(1) Reformed Spanish Ch., Schools, 8, Madera Baja. Rev. J. B. Cabrera.
(2) German Mission, 27, Calle de Calatrava ; also Schools, Orphanage, and Hospital. Director, Pastor Fliedner.   .
(3) United Presb. Mission, 4, Leganitos. Schools.
(4) Irish Presb. Mission. Schools, 57 and 59, Meson de Paredes.
(5) Methodist Mission, 68, Calle de Atocha.
(6) Brethren's Mission, 5, Glorieta de Quevedo, Chamberi. Schools.

MADRID :

B. and F. Bible Soc., 4, Leganitos. Agent, Rev. J. Jameson. Dépôt, 34, Preciados.

Rel. Tract Soc., 59, Jacomotrezo.

Home for Governesses.

MALAGA.—Ref. Sp. Ch., Rev. J. M. Vila. Dutch Mission, 149, Calle de Torrijos.

PUERTO STA. MARIA (Andalusia).—Missionary Training College (undenominational). Director, Rev. W. Moore, 62, Calle de Palacios.

REUS.— Ch. and Schools, 2, Calle de Vidal.

SALAMANCA.—Ref. Sp. Ch.

SAN FERNANDO.—Un. Presb. Mission. S. Bernardo, 55.

SAN SEBASTIAN.—Amer. Board. Rev. W. H. Gulick, 40, Avenida de la Libertad. Sp. and Engl. Boarding School.

SANTANDER.—Amer. Board, Ch. and Schools; 7, Cuesta del Hospital.

Seville.—C. and C.C.S. Ch. of the Ascension, Pl. Murillo.

Spanish Services : (1) Sp. Evang. Soc., Bustos Tavera, 33. (2) Ref. Sp. Ch. (a) San Basilio, Calle Relator. (b) Ch. of Assumption. (c) Triana. Church and Schools.

Miss Butcher, 27, San Vicente, Sunday and Day Schools.

Bible Soc. Dépôt, 134, Calle de la Feria.

VALLADOLID. — Ref. Sp. Ch. ; also stations in two villages. Brethren's Mission.

ZARAGOZA.—Amer. Board, 85, Calle San Pablo. Ch. and Schools.

PORTUGAL.

Population (1881), 4,306,554.

LISBON.—Epis. Ch., Rua Nova da Estrella, Rev. T. G. P. Pope. Free Presb. Ch., 2, Rua Direita Janellas Verdes, 11.30 and 6.30, Rev. A. D. Paterson.

Portuguese Services—Lusitanian Ch. : (1) S. Pedro, Largo das Taipas. (2) S. Paulo, 123, Rua Occidental da Moeda. (3) Rua da Conceiçao. (4) Rio de Mouro, near to Cintra.

Evangelical Portuguese Ch. Service in Presbyterian Ch. at 10 and 2.

Evangelical Congregation, 5, Largo do Cascao.

B. and F. Bible Society's Agent, Rev. R. Stewart. Dépôt, 32, Rua Direita Janellas Verdes.

Tract Dépôt, 32, Janellas Verdes.

Benevolent Institutions :
  (1) O. Hospital de S. José.
  (2)   Do.   Sta. Estephania (for women).
  (3) Real Casa Pia at Belem (for boys).
  (4) Casa de Correcçaò (Reformatory).
  (5) Asylo de Raparigas Abandonadas (for destitute girls).
  (6) Crèches in different parts of city.
  (7) Asylos de Infancia desvalida—several.

OPORTO.—Lusitanian Ch. :
  (1) Villa Nova da Gaya, Rev. Jas. Cassels.
  (2) Ch. of Redeemer, S. Lazaro.

Wesl. Ch., Largo do Cornel Paccheco. Mission Candal, Mr. R. H. Moreton. Mission Bom Successo, Mr. J. England.

B. and F. Bible Soc., and Religious Tract Soc., 29, Rua do Mousinho da Silveira.

AUSTRIA.

Population (1880) of Austro-Hungarian Monarchy, 37,882,712.

In Austria alone : Roman Catholics, 17,693,648 ; Greek Catholics, 2,536,177 ; Protestants, in 1885, 411,333 ; Jews, 1,005,394 ; Greek Ch. and Armenians, 493,542.

In Hungary, in 1880 : Roman Catholics, 7,849,692 ; Greek Catholics, 1,497,268 ; Eastern Greek Ch., 2,434,890 ;

Protestants (Lutherans, 1,122,849, Calvinists, 2,031,803, and Unitarians, 55,792), 3,210,444 ; Jews, 638,314. Baptists in Austria-Hungary, 4 chapels, 80 places where meetings are held, 1,288 members, and 651 S. scholars.

Lutherans in Moravia and Silesia, 104,949.

    „   Vienna district, 62,817.

    „   Lemberg district, 48,911.

    „   Bohemia, 32,148.

    „   Asch district, 23,518.

    „   Upper Austria, 17,707.

Reformed Ch., Bohemia, 69,533.

    „   Moravia, 40,055.

    „   Vienna district, 6,388.

The Oberkirchenrath is the ruling body of the Lutheran and Reformed Chs. of Austria. President, Dr. Rudolf Franz. Sec., Joseph Dobrowohay. Office : I. Schillerplatz, Vienna. One of the clerical members for Lutheran Ch. is Dr. Gustav Frank. One of the clerical members for Ref. Ch. is Dr. Hermann von Tardy.

Carlsbad (Bohemia).—C. and C.C.S., St. Luke's, various ; May to September.

Presb. Ch., July to September.

Bible and Tract Soc. Publications to be had at Feller's, Alte Wiese ; and at Knauer's, near Post Office.

CRACOW.—London Jews' Soc., Mr. Joseph Pick, Lubiczgasse, 36.

Cortina.—C. and C.C.S., Hot. Aquila Nera, various.

CZASLAU (Bohemia).—Teachers' Seminary.

DEBRECZIN.—Prot. University and Gymnasium, with 1,000 pupils. Profs. Balogh, Csiky, and others.

FELDKIRCHEN (Carinthia). — Orphanage. Director, Pastor Schwarz.

Franzensbad.—S.P.G., at Königs Villa, June and July.

Gmunden.—C. and C.C.S.

GRATZ (Styria).—Evangelistic Work, P. W. Reinmuth, 49, Naglergasse.

HRADISTE.—Nasawrky, Past. L. B. Kaspar, editor of Comenius Soc.

Innsbruck (Tyrol).—C. and C.C.S., Lieder Tafel, June to September, at 11 a.m.

Presb. Ch., July to September.

Ischl (Salzburg).—S.P.G., July to September.

KLAUSENBURG (Transylvania).—Bible Depôt, J. Rottmayer, 6, Kandiagasse.

KRABSCHITZ, near Raudnitz.—Bohemian Prot. Training Sch. for Girls. Director, Pastor Scholtez.

LEMBERG (Galicia).—Prot. Ch. Germ. Service at 10 a.m., but on second Sunday of month in Polish. British Jews' Society, Miss Pick, Ulica Hetmaieskagasse, 6. London Jews' Soc., Mr. M. Rosenstrauch, Ulica Syktuska, 64.
Dépôt B. and F. Bible Soc., 4, Copernicusgasse.

Marienbad (Bohemia).—S.P.G., Christchurch, May to September.

Meran (Tyrol).—S.P.G. Freihof Ch., Oct. to May, Rev. E. H. Noel. Germ. Prot. Ch., 10.

Pesth.—S.P.G., Hot. Hungaria, 10.30 to 4., Rev. R. Hake. Hungarian Ref. Ch., Calvinplatz. Lutheran Ch. (Hung. and German), Deakplatz. Free Ch. of Scotland Jewish Mission. Ministers—Rev. R. König, Engl's Villa, Stadtwäldchen ; Rev. A. Moody, 8, Rudolf Quai. Services in the Church, Mondgasse : German at 10 and 6. English, by Rev. A. Moody, at 11.30. French (at intervals) at 4. Mission School, 17, Mondgasse. Above 400 children, about half of them Jewish. Building belongs to Fr. Ch. of Scotland. Young Women's Christian Association in the Schoolhouse. Mgs. on Sunday (German) at 4.30.

Prot. Hosp., 'Bethesda,' Stadtwäldchen.

Governesses' Home (Home Suisse), Fabrikengasse, 18.

Bible Dépôt, M. Victor, 4, Deakplatz.

Tract Dépôt, Rev. R. König, Waiznerster, 76.

Bapt. (German) Services, 59, Königsgasse, 9 and 5. Minister, Mr. Meyer.

PRAGUE.—Free Ch. of Scotland, 7, Postgasse. English Service at 11, German Service at 5 p.m.

American Mission, Rev. A. W. Clark, Schwarzenbergstr., 62, Smichov. Places for Worship, Tischlergasse, 24, and 475, Mikovetegasse, im Weinberge. Services in Bohemian at 10 and 3. Services on Sunday evening in 6 suburbs.

Y.M.C.A., Martensgasse, 4.

B. and F. Bible Society, K. M. L. Stahlschmidt, 52, Wenzels-Platz.

Tract and Book Soc., M. J. Bastecky, Ferdinandstr., 9.

Baptist Service, 197, Jungmannsgasse, Vrsovic.

Free Ch. of Scotland Jewish Mission, Rev. Jas. Pirie, 352, Smichov.

Heimat (Home for Girls). President, Rev. A. W. Clark, Branik, near Prague.

Riva zur Garda See. S.P.G., June and Oct.

Salzburg (Tyrol).—C. and C.C.S., at Germ. Prot. Ch.

SERAJEVI (Bosnia).—B. and F. Bible Society's Dépôt. A. Hempt, 2, H. Durakofgasse.

Trent (Tyrol).—C. and C.C.S.

Trieste (Istria).—Engl. Episc. Ch., 11 and 6.

German Prot. Churches, Ref. and Lutheran.

B. and F. Bible Society, 3, Via Ponte Rosso.

Vienna.—Engl. Ch. Services. Embassy Chapel, 6, Metternichgasse, at 11, Rev. W. H. Hechler.

Free Ch. of Scotland, 9, Eschenbachgasse, at 11. Rev. F. Gordon. Sept. to June.

German Lutheran Services, 1 Dorotheergasse, 18 (formerly Ch. of St. Mary, Queen of Angels), at 10 and 5, Children's Service at 3.

Ref. Ch. Services (German), 16, Dorotheergasse (also a part of the King's Monastery, to which the Lutheran Ch. also formerly belonged), at 10, Instruction of Children 8.45 to 9.45 a.m. French Service in same place at 12.

Wesl. Ch. Service, Dreilaufergasse, 15 (only invited persons can by law attend).

VIENNA :

Baptist Meetings, 7, Breitegasse, at 9.30 and 5 (only invited persons can by law attend).

Protestant Theological Faculty (1822), Dr. E. Böhl (Dogmatics and Symbolics, Ref. Ch.), Dr. W. Frank (do., Luth. Ch.), and 4 other professors.

B. and F. Bible Society. Agent, Mr. Henry E. Millard, Elisabethstr., 6.

Scottish Bible Soc. Agent, Mr. Priggen, I. Getreidemarkt, 4.

Religious Tract Society, I. Elisabethstr., 6.

Y.M.C.A., Mostgasse, 8a, IV.

London Jews' Soc., Rev. G. H. Händler, Salzgries, 18, IV. Stock.

British Jews' Soc., Rev. C. A. Schönberger, I. Salzgries, 12, III. Stock ; and Mr. E. Weiss, 5, Bez Pilgrimgasse, 15, IV. Stock, Thr, 12.

Home for Swiss Governesses, Miss de Blairville, I. Himmelpfortgasse, 20. Also English Home for ditto, Weihburggasse, 16, I.

N.B.—Stations of Ev. Contl. Soc. at Horjitz, Laun, etc. For information, inquire of Rev. A. W. Clark, Prag.

DENMARK.

Population in 1880, 1,969,039. In 1880, Lutherans, 1,951,361 ; Reformed, 1,363 ; Rom. Catholics, 2,985 ; Baptists, 22 churches, 2,369 members, and 2,225 S. scholars ; Jews, 3,946 ; and Mormons, 1,722.

American Meth. Episc. Ch.—4 ordained Danish preachers, 810 members, and 1,346 S. scholars.

Salvation Army, stations in 5 towns, including Copenhagen, Aalborg, and Odensee.

Copenhagen.—Engl. Episc. Ch., 21, Stormgade, 11.

Ref. Ch., French and German Services alternately, 10 and 1, at 171, Gothersgade.

Meth. Episc. Ch., Riegensgade.

COPENHAGEN :
Salvation Army, headquarters, Zinsgade, 3 ; 4 stations.
Danish Agencies : 1. Bible Soc. 2. Miss. Soc. (Greenland and India) ; Secretary, Rev. A. Holm, Gladsaxe, near Copenhagen. 3. Home Missions — (*a*) for Copenhagen ; Secretary, Rev. H. Stein, Frydsvej ; Mission-house in Römersgade. (*b*) For Denmark ; Secretary, Rev. W. Beck, Udby Slagelse. Lay-preachers sent to all parts of the country. 4. Society for Sunday Observance ; Secretary, Dr. K. Westergaard. 5. Bethel-ship for Sailors ; Secretary, Rev. D. Prior.
Institute for Deaf, Dumb, and Blind, Citadelsnej.
Deaconesses' Institute, 50 Smellegade.
B. and F. Bible Society. Agent, Rev. J. Plenge, 79, Vesterbrogade and Friederiksborggade.
FREDERIKSHAVN.—Meth. Episc. Ch.
NORRE ALSLEV (Falster).—Tract Dépôt, Rev. Provost Vahl.
SVENDBORG.—Meth. Episc. Ch.

NORWAY.

Population (1875), 1,806,900. Lutherans (State Ch.), 1,799,662 ; Free Ch. Lutheran, 1,184 ; Methodists, 2,759 ; Roman Catholics, 502 ; Baptists, 1,389 members and 1,325 S. scholars ; Salvation Army stations in 11 towns ; Jews, 34.
American Meth. Episc. Miss. Soc., 28 ordained preachers, 3,261 members, and 3,381 S. scholars.
Free Ch. (mixed Congl. and Presb.) 12 churches, 7 ministers, and 1,500 members.
ARENDAL.—Free Ch., 10 and 5. Episc. Meth. Ch. Bapt. Mission.
Bergen.—C. and C.C.S., Old Museum Sch., 11.
Baptist Mission. Episc. Meth. Ch.
Sailors' Mission. Secretary, Rev. J. Aars, Nicolaysen.
B. and F. Bible Soc. Dépôt, Mr. C. J. Mohn.

Christiania.—Engl. Episc. Ch., at Mission House.
Free Ch., 10 and 5. Pastor Tallaksen, 29, Toftesgade.
Episc. Meth. and Moravian Chs.
Salvation Army, headquarters, Gronland, 9 ; 3 stations.
Gymnastic Hall, near the Castle. Preaching at 11 on
Sunday by Pastor J. S. Munk.
Lutherstiftelsen : (a) Home Mission ; Secretary, Rev.
Kr. Mart. Eckhoff. (b) Tracts, Rev. J. G. Blom.
Dépôt at the Boghandel, Nedve, Slotsgade, 13.
B. and F. Bible Society's Dépôt at Messrs. Groendahl's,
Toldbodgade.
Deaconesses' Institute, Miss Guldberg.
Y.M.C.A. Secretary, Rev. Kr. Mart. Eckhoff.
CHRISTIANSAND.—Free Ch., 10 and 6. Episc. Meth. Ch.
Bapt. Mission.
B. and F. Bible Soc. Dépôt, Mr. T. Siqveland.
Drondheim.—C. and C.C.S., The Chapter House. Mora-
vian Ch. Bapt. Mission. Episc. Meth. Ch. Town
Mission, Pastor M. Giverholdt.
B. and F. Bible Soc. Dépôt, M. P. Ulstad.
Eide.—C. and C.C.S.
Fagernoes.—C. and C.C.S.
Faleide on Nord Fiord.—S.P.G., July and Aug.
Honefoss.—C. and C.C.S.
Laerdalsoern.—S.P.G., June 15 to Aug 31.
Molde.—C. and C.C.S.
Molde (Romsdal).—S.P.G., July to Aug.
Naes, near Romsdalen.—S.P.G., July and Aug.
Odde (Hardanger Fiord).—S.P.G., June 15 to Aug. 31.
STAVANGER.—Moravian and Quaker Chs.
Norwegian Soc. for Missions. Secretary, Rev. O.
Gjerlöw.
B. and F. Bible Society's Dépôt. M. Lars Oftedal.
TROMSO.—B. and F. Bible Society's Dépôt. M. J.
Killengreen.

SWEDEN.

Population (1887), 4,734,901. Lutherans (1880), 4,544,434; Roman Catholics, 810; Jews, 2,993; Baptists, 18 associations, 473 churches, 31,849 members, and 31,273 S. scholars; Meth. Episc. Ch., 50 ordained native preachers, 8,814 members, and 8,718 S. scholars.

Salvation Army stations in 47 towns.

GOTHENBURG.—Methodist Episcopal Ch. and Moravian Ch.

Salvation Army, Concert du Boulevard, and 2 other stations.

KARLSKRONA.—Meth. Episc. Ch.

Stockholm.—C. and C.C.S., St. Peter and Siegfrid, 24, Rörstrandsgatan, 11.

German Ch., Swartmangatan, 11.

French Ch., 15, Sôdra Humlegardsgatan, 11.

Moravian Ch., 12, Ostra Trudgardsgatan.

Meth. Episc. Ch., 20., Rôrstrandsgatan.

Bapt. Ch., 48, D. Malmskīlnadsgatan, 11 and 6.

Salvation Army, headquarters, Ostermalmsgatan, 33, and 4 stations.

Y.M.C.A., 2, Kungsgatan.

Swedish Miss. Soc. Pastor H. W. Totlie (Upsala), Secretary.

City Mission. G. S. Lowenhjelm, Chairman, 34, Nybrogatan.

Evang. National Soc. (Evangeliska Fosterlands Stiftelser), comprising Home and Foreign Missions, Seamen's Mission, and Bible and Tract Dépôt, 34, Mäster Samuelsgatan. Pastor Arnström, Secretary.

Tract Dépôt, M. Olaf Janzon, Evangeliska Fosterlands Stiftelsen's Expedition.

Baptist Tract Dépôt, Luntmakaregatan, 5.

STOCKHOLM :
Deaconesses' Institution, Stora Ersta.
Ragged School Home, Sôdra Bangârdsgatan, 12.
Homes or Refuges for Young Women in several parts
of Stockholm.
Baron Barnekow's Night Refuge for Men, David
Bagaregata.
Crèches exist and flourish in several parishes.

RUSSIA.

Population in Europe (including Poland), 89,685,489.

Greek Church,   about ...   ... 60,000,000.
Roman Catholics,   „   ...   ... 7,500,000.
Protestant Church, „   ...   ... 2,800,000.
Jews,   „   ...   ... 2,600,000.

Finland, population in 1886, 2,232,378, mostly
Lutherans.
Baptists, 32 churches, 10,110 members, and 2,835 S.
scholars.
CHARKOFF.—Bible Dépôt, Ekaterinoslaffskaya.
HELSINGFORS.—Bible Dépôt, Captain H. Fagerlund, 4,
Mariegatan.
Tract Dépôt, Miss Sahlberg.
KAZAN.—Bible Dépôt, Mr. E. Kirsch, Suburb-street.
KIEFF.—Bible Dépôt, Alexandroffskaya-street.
KISHINEFF.—London Jews' Society, Rev. R. Faltin,
the Rectory. Herr Rabinowitch's Judeo-Christian
Ch.
Moscow.—English Church, Great Tshernishoff-lane.
Pastor Waiberg. Services, 11 and 7.
Evangl. Ref. Ch., Tryochsvyatetlni-lane, 11 and 8.
Service alternately in French and German. Pastor
Prinzhorn.
German-Luth. Ch., St. Michael's Church, 10.30.
German-Luth. Ch., St. Peter and Paul Church, Kos-
modemyanski-lane, 10.30.

Moscow :

British and Foreign Bible Society's Depositary, Mr. C. Holmström, Tretyäkoffski-passage, Nikolski-street.

Odessa.—Eng. Episc. Ch., Dom Wagner, Rev. E. W. Wagner.

Eng. Ref. Ch. Service alternately in French and German.

B. and F. Bible Society's Agent, Mr. M. A. Morrison, Chersonskistz, 58.

Riga.—English Church, Anglikanische Strasse.

German Luth. Churches, the Cathedral and St. Peter's Church, 10.

German Reformed Church, 10.

German Baptist Ch., 10, Felliner-str., 10 and 4.

Lettish Baptist Ch., Hagensberg, Tempel-str.

B. and F. Bible Society's Dépôt, Mr. A. Weismann, 9, Théâtre Boulevard.

St. Petersburg.—Brit. and Amer. Chapel, Rev. J. D. Kilburn, 16, New Isaac-street, 11 and 6.30.

Engl. Congl. Ch., Alexandroffsky, Rev. James Key. Services, 11 and 6.30.

German Ref. Ch., Pastor Gelderblom, Gr. Morskaya. 10.30.

German Lutheran Churches : St. Peter's, 20, Nevsky Prospect, 10.30. St. Ann's, Litennie Prospect, 10.30. St. Katherine's, Wassily Ostr., 1 line, 10.30. St. Michael's, Wassily Ostr., 3 line.

German Luth. Evgl. Hospital.

Evgl. Luth. Churches : St. Mary's, Petersburger Side. Service alternately German and Russian, 10.30. Jesus Church. Service alternately Lettish and German. German Evgl. Luth. Church, St. George's, Petersburg-Side.

French Ref. Ch., 25, Gt. Koniushennaya, at 11.

Moravian Ch., 24, New Isaac-street.

Baptist Ch., Pryadilnaya-street, 15, Quartier 6, at 10.30.

St. Petersburg :
  B. and F. Bible Society's Agent, Rev.W. Nicolson, M.A.,
    4, New Isaac-street.
  Tract Dépôt, Mr. F. A. Grote, 24, Little Morskaya.
Saratof.—B. and F. Bible Society's Dépôt, Mr. Peter
    Perk, Moscow-street House, Inshakavoi.
Tiflis. — Bible Dépôt, Golovinsky, Prospect House
    Zubaloff.
Warsaw.—Engl. Episc. Ch., 17, Smolna-street, 11.
  Lutheran Ch. (German), 15, Krulewska, 10 and 4.
  Ref. Ch., 16, Leszno, alternately every Sunday, German
    and Polish Services, at 10 a.m.
  Population 401,000 ; of these 129,240 are Jews and
    18,573 Protestants.
  London Jews' Soc., Rev. O. J. Ellis, D.D., 1, Szpitalna.
  B. and F. Bible Soc. Dépôt, A. Kantor, 2, Senatoren-
    street.
  Tract Dépôt, Mr. Stefan Lasocki, Leszno 20
  Baptist Ch., 12, Chlodna, 9 and 4.
  The Plochocin Orphanage, near Warsaw, is under the
    care of a converted Israelite.
Wilna.—British Jews' Soc., Rev. G. Friedman, Pre-
    demestjé Nowi Swjet House, Pitalewa. Dr. Frohwein,
    Bakschta-street House, Ganstein.

TURKEY AND GREECE.

Turkey, population of actual possessions, 4,500,000.
Greece, population in 1879, 1,979,561.
Bosnia and Herzegovina (occupied by Austria), popula-
    tion 1,336,091.
Sandjak Novi Bazar (occupied by Austria), 168,000.
Montenegro, population 236,000.
The European Turkey Mission of American Board has
4 stations and 27 out-stations, 10 missionaries, and 444
members.

ADRIANOPLE.—Brit. Jews' Soc. Rev. L. Rosenberg.

ATHENS.—Evngl. Greek Mission and Publications. Rev. Dr. Kalopothakes. Services and S. schools also at Piræus and Volo. Baptist Mission—3 native preachers and 7 members.

Bible Dépôt. — Rev. Dr. Kalopothakes, 39, Odos Stadion.

Constantinople.—*English Services:*

(1) Ch. of Engl. Embassy, Pera, at 10.30 and 5. In the summer these services are transferred to Therapia on the Bosphorus.

(2) Christ Ch. in lower part of Pera, at 11. Rev. C. G. Curtis.

(3) Ch. of the Dutch Embassy, Pera. Preaching by Rev. Jas. Henderson, of Free Ch. of Scotland, at 3 p.m., Nov. to April.

(4) Engl. Ch. at Bebek on Bosphorus. Preaching by American Missionaries and others, at 11.

(5) Engl. Episc. Ch. at Kadikeuy on the Marmora, 11 and 7.30.

(6) Hasskeuy on Golden Horn. Engl. Episc Ch. at 6, in connection with London Jewish Mission.

(7) Hasskeuy. Presb. Ch. at 11, in connection with Mission to the Jews of the Established Church of Scotland.

(8) Robert College on the Bosphorus. Engl. Services at 10.45, 3 and 7.30, for the benefit of the students, but open to all.

(9) American Ch., Scutari — Selamsuz quarter — at Home School (public).

Religious Services, conducted mostly by native pastors and preachers, are held every Sunday in the Turkish language, in a building adjoining Bible House, and also in Lauga Chapel, Stamboul; in Greek at the Bible House Ch. and at the Dutch Embassy Ch., Pera ; and in Armenian at the Lauga Ch. at Upper or Armenian Hasskeuy and Scutari.

CONSTANTINOPLE :

Educational and Benevolent Institutions :

(1) Robert College at Roumeli Hissar on Bosphorus. President, Rev. George Washburn, D.D.

(2) An Orphanage and a Girls' Home in same connection.

(3) A Medical Mission and Dispensary for Jews aud others at Scotch Mission House in Galata.

(4) Mission Schs. for Jews of London Soc. and Ch. of Scotland in Hasskeuy.

Evangelical Christian Work ı

(1) Agencies of American Bible Soc. under Rev. Dr. L. G. Bliss ; and of B. and F. Bible Soc. under Rev. Dr. Thomson ; and of American Board of Foreign Missions at Bible House, Stamboul, midway between the Karakeuy Bridge and the Seraskier's Tower.

(2) American Board in European Turkey (A.B.C.F.M.). Directors, Rev. Dr. Rigg and others, Constantinople. Works wholly among Bulgarians. 4 stations and 29 out-stations, 8 churches, 9 American missionaries, and 1 medical missionary, 14 lady missionaries, 6 Bulgarian pastors and 11 preachers, 20 teachers, 650 Church members, 23 S. schools with 1,251 pupils. Theol. Seminary, 12 students. In Collegiate Institute, 61 pupils ; 2 Girls' High Schools, 76 pupils ; 11 day schools, 423 pupils ; and 10 Bible-women. Contributions in 1888, nearly £725.

(3) The Mission of Free Ch. of Scotland to the Jews, Mission House, Galata, Perehambé, Bazaar Street, near the Tower. Missionaries, Revs. J. Tomory, J. Henderson and R. Hannington.

(4) Mission to the Jews of Established Ch. of Scotland, Hasskeuy.

(5) Mission of London Jews' Society, Rev. J. B. C. Ginsburg, Yali Sokak, 9, Ortakeuy.

CONSTANTINOPLE :

(6) At No. 44, Rue Voivoide, Galata, is a Rest (Café and Reading Room), a centre of Christian work.

(7) A Medical Mission in Stamboul (the old city) under charge of Gabriel S. Dobrashian, M.D. The Mission is designed especially for Armenians, and has connected with it a day school in the city and an industrial school at Baghtchejik.

JOANNINA (S. Albania).—B. and F. Bible Soc., Mr. N. J. Discus, Stamboul Bible Dépôt.

MONASTIR (Macedonia).—A.B.C.F.M. Revs. Lewis Bond and W. E. Locke.

B. and F. Bible Soc. Dépôt. Mr. G. D. Kyrias.

Patras.—S.P.G., with Zante. Rev. F. G. Mitchell.

SALONICA.—Scottish Natl. Bible Soc. Dépôt at house of Rev. P. Crosbie. Also missionary to Jews.

Mission of American Southern Presbyterian Church, with school and preaching places.

SCUTARI (North Albania).—B. and F. Bible Society's Dépôt. M. A. Serfurd.

VOLO (Thessaly).—B. and F. Bible Soc. Dépôt. Rev. D. Liaoutses.

BULGARIA AND E. ROUMELIA.

Population, 3,154,375.

American Board Foreign Mission. For statistics, see under Constantinople, Evangl. Christian work.

Methodist Episcopal Church Statistics : 4 foreign missionaries, 14 native missionaries, 144 members, and 116 adherents ; 1 theological and high school with 28 students, 1 girls' high school with 30 pupils, and 4 day schools with 88 pupils.

LOFTCHA.—Meth. Episc. Ch. Rev. D. C. Challis, Supt. of Mission in Bulgaria.

LOMPALANKA-ON-DANUBE.—Resident Colporteur of B. and F. Bible Soc. Jakob Klundt.

ORCHANIA.—Meth. Episc. Ch. Pastor, Stephan Get-choff.

PHILIPPOPOLIS.—A.B.C.F.M. Rev. G. D. Marsh, and Pastor J. A. Tonjoroff ; Miss E. M. Stone directs Bible-women. Also American Publication Work.

PLEVNA.—Meth. Episc. Ch. Y. Tswettkoff.

RUSTCHUK.—Meth. Episc. Ch. Revs. E. F. Loundsbury and J. S. Ladd.
B. and F. Bible Dépôt. Mr. C. Krzossa.

SAMOKOV.—Station of A.B.C.F.M. Revs. J. F. Clarke, Dr. J. H. House, Dr. Haskell, and T. L. Kingsbury, M.D.
Collegiate Inst., with Industrial Dept.

SELVI.—Meth. Episc. Ch. G. Elieff.

SISTOF.—Meth. Episc. Ch. Pastor, S. Thomoff. Rev. J. S. Ladd, Principal of Theological School.

SOPHIA.—Bulgarian Evang. Soc., aided by A.B.C.F.M. Pastor N. T. Boyadjieff.

VARNA.—Meth. Episc. Ch. T. Constantine.

ROUMANIA.

Population, 5,376,000.

Baptists, 5 chapels, and 200 members.

Bucharest.—English Services, 10.45.
German Lutheran Ch., 10. Bapt. Mg. at 25, Strada Italiano, 10 and 4.45.
B. and F. Bible Society's Dépôt, D. Schwegler, 51, Calea Mosilor.

JASSY.—Lutheran Ch.

SERVIA.

Population in 1887, 2,013,691 ; of these 153,560 speak Rouman, 29,020 Bohemian, and the rest Serb.

BELGRADE.—B. and F. Bible Soc. Dépôt. W. Lichten-berger, 52, Pop Lukinaulice.

BOOKS MOSTLY REFERRED TO.

EUROPE.

GENERAL STATE OF RELIGION.

Series of Articles in *Congregationalist* in 1876-7, by Rev. R. S. Ashton, B.A.

'Abriss der Geschichte der Evangelischen Kirche auf dem Europ. Festlande im 19ten Jahrhundert,' von Ad. Zahn. Stuttgart, 1886.

'Hist. de la Réformation en Europe,' par Merle d'Aubigné, 8 tomes. Lévy, Paris.

FRANCE.

STATE OF RELIGION, EVANGELIZATION, ETC.

'White Fields of France,' Hor. Bonar, D.D. Nisbet.

'Cry from Land of Calvin and Voltaire,' Hor. Bonar, D.D. Hodder and Stoughton.

'Cinquantenaire de le Soc. Evangélique de France, 1833-1883.' Paris.

'Yesterday and To-day; or, Activities of French Protestants,' by Westphal-Castelnau. Paris, 1885.

'Récits et Souvenirs, 1831-1881.' Béroud, Genève, 1882.

La Charité Privée à Paris,' par Max. du Camp. Hachette, Paris, 1886.

HISTORY OF PROTESTANTISM.

Histoire des Protestants du France,' par G. de Félice. Grassart, Paris.

'Histoire de la Réformation Française,' par F. Puaux, 7 tomes. Agence Ecoles du Dim, Paris.

'Récits du 16me Siècle,' 1re and 2me Séries, par Jules Bonnet. Grassart, Paris.

'Nouveaux Récits,' do.

'Derniers Récits,' do.

'Hist. des Protestants de France depuis 1861,' F. Bonifas. Toulouse, Soc. Livres Religieux, 1874.

'Mémoires du Réveil Religieux,' par A. Bost, 3 vols. Grassart, Paris, 1855.

'Les Premiers Pasteurs du Désert,' par O. Douen, 2 tomes. Grassart, Paris, 1879.

BELGIUM.

'Hist. de la Soc. Evangélique Belge,' par L. Anet. Bruxelles, 1875.

'Corn-Seed in Belgium,' by R. H. Lundie. Nisbet, 1880.

GERMANY.

'Leitfaden der Inneren Mission,' von Theod. Schäfer. Rauhe Haus, Hamburg, 1887.

'Werk der Inneren Mission in d. Evang. Kirche der Rheinprovinz,' von H. Höpfner. Bonn, 1876.

'Praying and Working,' W. F. Stevenson. Strahan.

'Charities of Europe,' De Liefde.

'Homes and Haunts of Luther,' by Dr. Stoughton. Rel. Tr. Society.

History of Reformation in 16th century,' Dr. Merle d'Aubigné. Rel. Tr. Soc.

AUSTRIA.

'Conférence de Genève en 1861 ' (Evang. Alliance), Vol. II. Paper by Fred. de Rougemont. H. Georg, Genève.
'Das Evangelische Wien,' von Dr. Witz. Hartleben, Wien, 1887.

RUSSIA.

'Evangelische Strömungen in der Russischen Kirche der Gegenwart,' H. Dalton. Heilbronn, 1881.

BOHEMIA.

'Gospel in Bohemia,' E. Jane Whately. Rel. Tr. Soc.
'Destruction du Protestantisme en Bohème,' par R. Reuss. Strasbourg, 1868.

ITALY.

'Hist. des Vaudois d'Italie,' par Em. Comba. Fischbacher, Paris.
'Annuario Evangelico,' published every year, 51, Via de' Serragli, Florence.
'L'Italie Actuelle,' par E. de Laveleye. Hachette, Londres, 1880.
'Nouvelles Lettres d'Italie,' par E. de Laveleye. Baillière, Paris, 1884.
'Footprints of the Italian Reformers,' Dr. Stoughton. Rel. Tr. Soc.

SPAIN.

'Dawn of Second Reformation in Spain,' Mrs. R. Peddie. Partridge and Co.
'Manuel Matamoros,' W. Greene. J. Snow and Co.
'Footprints of the Spanish Reformers,' Dr. Stoughton. Rel. Tr. Soc.

CONTINENTAL SUNDAY SCHOOLS.

Persons willing to give information :

(1) Germany—Ct. A. von Bernstorf, 5, Ranstrasse, Berlin.

Rev. J. Rohrbach, 58, Bremerstr. Moabit, Berlin, N.W.

Rev. J. G. Fetzer, Horn, Hamburg.

Rev. Dr. Bickel, 98, Mittelweg, Berg-felde, Hamburg.

(2) France—Mons. Sautter, 12, Av. de l'Alma, Paris.

(3) Switzerland—Rev. S. Jaulmes Cook, 5, Beless Riches, Lausanne.

(4) Holland—Mr. J. M. Heybrook, 62, Rosengracht, Amsterdam.

(5) Denmark—Rev. H. Ussing, Veilby per Aarhuis.

(6) Sweden—Mr. Palm, 40, Malmkilnadsgaten, Stock-holm.

Pastor Truva, Gothenburg.

Pastor E. G. Lazergren, Sundsvall.

Pastor Backmanne, Orebro.

THE END.

Elliot Stock, Paternoster Row, London.

www.ingramcontent.com/pod-product-compliance
Lightning Source LLC
Chambersburg PA
CBHW032358280326

41935CB00008B/623